THIS SIDE OF JESUS
— IN THE SECRET PLACE

Printed and bound by Print Solutions Partnership, Wallington, Surrey, England

Published by Crossbridge Books
345 Old Birmingham Road
Bromsgrove B60 1NX
Tel: 0121 447 7897
www.crossbridgebooks.com

© Diana Holmes 2005

First published 2005

All rights reserved. No part of this publication may be reproduced, stored in a retrieval system or transmitted in any form or by any means — electronic, mechanical, photocopying, recording or otherwise — without prior permission of the Publisher.

ISBN 0 9549708 1 0

British Library Cataloguing in Publication Data. A catalogue record for this book is available from the British Library.

Also published by Crossbridge Books:

It's True! Trevor Dearing (Imprint: **Mohr Books**)
Total Healing Trevor Dearing (Imprint: **Mohr Books**)
The God of Miracles Trevor and Anne Dearing
First Century Close-ups Roger Penney
Schizophrenia Defeated James Stacey
Mountains on the Moon Michael Arthern
Then Something Remarkable Happened! Ron Jones

COVER BY ROLF MOHR

THIS SIDE OF JESUS
— IN THE SECRET PLACE

DIANA HOLMES

CROSSBRIDGE BOOKS

DEDICATED TO THE GLORY OF GOD

Lamentations 3: 25

The Lord is good
To those who wait for Him,
To the soul who seeks Him.

BIBLICAL QUOTATIONS are taken from the
New International Version of the Holy Bible,
unless otherwise indicated (See p. 219).

INTRODUCTION

The introduction must start long before I knew that the Lord had conceived this book.

Over a period of twenty-three years I was misdiagnosed with six different diseases and treated for them all. The diseases are namely: epilepsy, coeliac disease (allergy to the protein in wheat and rye), polymyalgia rheumatica, (a muscular disease — treated with high doses of steroids), depression, M.E. and last but not least myasthenia gravis (a very grave muscle disease — again treated with high doses of steroids). I saw many doctors and specialists over the years and none of them were able to help me. In the end I had to use a wheelchair. Finally I visited a private doctor who diagnosed me correctly with an underactive thyroid condition. I BECAME WELL!

I had had blood tests for thyroid function carried out but they were always returned, "in the normal range". My last set of blood test results were in the middle of the range and yet I had been diagnosed as hypothyroid (an underactive thyroid gland). I reasoned that if this had happened to me then it most certainly would have happened to other people. I carried out research and found that there was a flaw with the interpretation of the blood test results. I wrote reports, co-authored a medical paper, manned a help-line, assisted at thyroid clinics and wrote a book about my journey through illness to wellbeing. Thousands of people have stated that my story is their story. I knew that this was the work that the Lord wanted me to do.

I was diagnosed correctly in 1994 and the beginnings of this book 'This Side of Jesus — In the Secret Place' start in the year 2000. In that year I started to have visions of the Lord Jesus. He took me on "walks" and gave me sound teaching and new revelations. I thought they were very private and just for me personally, but very gently the Lord guided me to write them down. With these walks I found out who I was in Christ Jesus.

WHO AM I IN CHRIST JESUS?

I am loved unconditionally by the Lord — It is not by good deeds or service to the Lord God that He gives me His unconditional love, but purely by His grace. **Ephesians 2: 8-9**.

I am grafted into the seed of Abraham — The Lord God promised Abraham that He would make his descendants a great nation. **Genesis 12: 2** (NKJ)

I am a son/daughter of God Almighty —God sent His only Son Jesus to rescue (redeem) us from slavery into sonship (adoption). **Galatians 4: 4-7** (NKJ)

All my sins are forgiven — Once I recognised that Christ Jesus died for my sins and I repented of them, my sins were automatically forgiven. For my part I must try not to sin.

I am promised eternal life with Him. — **John 3: 16.**

God has a plan for my life on earth — God's plan for me is to bring the whole truth to the people.
Ephesians 2: 10

My freedom comes when I imitate Christ Jesus — If in all circumstances I could behave as Jesus would behave my life would not be complicated. I am learning, but it takes time.
2 Corinthians 3: 17-18

The thyroid work was fraught with jealousies, resentments, obstructions and accusations and these were from groups who were supposed to be working towards the same goal. There were hostilities even in the church. I knew that even though these things were happening to me I must carry on with the work. Sometimes I nearly walked away from it, but in the back of my mind I knew that I couldn't. This book takes the reader through the hurt and the pain with Jesus at my side.

Also my marriage was in trouble and the Lord showed me His love and caring.

I knew instinctively that I was in 'Spiritual Warfare'.

WHAT IS SPIRITUAL WARFARE?

Whenever we submit to Christ Jesus we will be under spiritual attack — spiritual warfare. It is how we react that matters. For example, if you receive an accusatory or a particularly hurtful letter from someone, the key is to leave it for a few days before you reply, if indeed you need to reply.

Because I stand for the truth, I have been through these hurtful experiences on many occasions. They come in the form of letters, emails, or telephone calls. I did not answer any of them. I am not saying that I wasn't offended, hurt and angry with these people — I most certainly was, but Jesus brought me through. If I had tried to defend myself, the hurts would have grown out of all proportion. At all times Jesus knows the truth.
    And we must remember that not many people have the courage to say hurtful things to your face.

    Jesus took me through the worst times with conviction, correction and discipline, gentleness, healing and love — most of all love. Love was at every turn.
    To become deep rooted in Christ I have to endure all that is thrown at me and LEARN patience and humility. It doesn't come easy.

The teaching in those walks was simple and that, I believe, is how the Lord wants us to spread His Word: with simplicity.

Sometimes in the walks I become as a child and then an adult. This is yet another message for me too – to be as a child before our God: "Abba" "Father".

In the following pages I share these walks with the reader. Each walk is dated; some state my thoughts before entering upon a walk and with some I discuss my thoughts in the interpretation.

The particular growth period for me in these walks is the realisation that I must die to self, *"die to the flesh"*, which is a process that is ongoing. Nearly every day I have to die to the flesh. I have already stated that I didn't give in to self and reply to the accusatory letters and emails. For those who have not been through it, it is a very painful experience but the benefit of not rising to the bait is freedom in its very essence and together with a knowledge that you are in the will of the Father.

WHAT IS "DYING TO THE FLESH"?

We have to die to the flesh in many areas of our life. I will outline a few:

a. We must remain immune to hurts thrown at us and remain in the Father's will.
b. Stand firm in the faith.
c. Refrain from asking the Lord for things that won't really help us in our walk with Him.
d. Put other people before ourselves.
e. Refrain from trying to move our spouses along in their walk with the Lord.

There are many more areas of dying to the flesh — far too many for this introduction. Wherever we are in life there will always be those who attack for no reason. The Lord wants us to die to the flesh. If we don't we become selfish. From selfish comes the anagram 'flesh is'.

    I wrote the prayer below to help me realise the stages that I have come through, and will go through again, and the goals to attain. The first stage is when I was in the midst of the hurt and pain, and ignorant in the knowledge of the Lord. I would need to overcome the hurdle of the pain of being hurt and let go certain things in my life.

> *How many times have the arrows pierced*
> *Emotionally in my mind*
> *Each arrowhead with each evil deed*
> *Might as well have been signed*
> *Each resentment struck shot speedily home*
> *From the bearer of hate from whence it was sown.*

> *Through knowledge of His Word*
> *I can see the Lord's face;*
> *I show Him hurt and pain*
> *And He shows His grace.*

> *The pain of letting go the hurt*
> *Is almost overwhelming;*
> *But for me there is no other resort*
> *Only then will my soul start mending.*

> *I know that to the flesh I must die*
> *And then will I reap my reward.*

I must not take account of the lies;
Instead, use the double-edged sword.

With freedom of the flesh
I gain a joy in the Lord in His will.
Forever more He reigns
But to know Him I must be still.

The Lord wants everyone to have a one to one relationship with Him. It doesn't come easily; it takes time and effort. To spend time alone with the Lord is precious. Sometimes just being in front of Him with no expectations of this prayer being answered or that prayer being answered. Just to thank Him for blessings. A relationship is a two-way thing. I called out to Jesus and He came. He will come to you, maybe not in the same way, but He will come. He is always there by our side — all we have to do is seek Him.

Thank you Father for your precious Word.

The Father's WORD is the:

W ay
O f
R esurrected
D ivinity.

Diana Holmes 2005

THIS SIDE OF JESUS
IN THE SECRET PLACE

Psalm 27:5 *For, in the time of trouble*
He shall hide me in His pavilion;
In the secret place of His tabernacle
He shall hide me;
He shall set me high upon a rock..

10th APRIL 2000

I put on my favourite CD of gentle classical music. My favourite track being Chopin – Nocturne in B Flat Minor. My Uncle Alfred used to play this and many more pieces for me when, as a child, I went to stay with him and my Aunt Elsie.

This gentle piano playing now soothed my soul. I wanted to be full of the Spirit of Jesus. I wanted to meet with Jesus in the inner part of me, the spirit part of me and to do that I had to be on my own in *'the secret place'*.

This secret place gave me my quiet time with Jesus. For some months now I had been crying out to Him. My marriage was in trouble and the work I was involved in was creating all sorts of problems. I closed my eyes and bowed my head, and kept repeating very quietly,

Jesus

Jesus

Jesus

A picture in my mind started to form — I found myself on a pathway, and in front of me stood Jesus. Instinctively I knew it was Jesus. I could see the back of his flowing robe. His hair was golden brown. He turned and beckoned me with His hand. I was completely unafraid. In fact I felt warmth spread through my whole body.

All the times when I had cried out, in anguish, to Jesus I could not feel His presence through my tears, and yet now when I whisper His name gently — I see Him.

I moved towards Him and placed my hand in His. Jesus led me into the most beautiful garden that I have ever seen. The sunlight sparkled like diamonds through the trees. There was such beauty around me. The birds' wondrous songs filled the air with their sweet music and the flowing water was likened to a full orchestra of sound, and I had my hand in the hand of the Gardener.

INTERPRETATION: The Lord was showing me the beauty of His creation. I was at peace. In my heart I know that I must trust and obey the Lord completely in everything I do. When I trust and obey Him I know such joy.

Sometimes I am so caught up in everything else that I forget to trust Him. By seeking out the beauty of His creation and taking time out to *'be'* I am led once more into His joy and His peace. We sometimes forget the beauty of God's creation and His will for us and easily get caught up in our own agenda, and the work we are involved in becomes the master.

There is only one Master – the Lord Jesus. Sometimes our work for the Lord demands our time and energy but it must be in the Lord's strength. If we try to do things in our own strength we fail in our endeavours and we are out of God's peace.

The world today has become enslaved to the intellectual and therefore balance is lacking. The Lord has given the gift of intellect to each one of us; but we mustn't let it become the master. Inside each one of us is a soul that needs nurturing to maturity.

Through this short walk with Jesus I became aware that my root must be wholly in Him for me to mature. It really doesn't matter what I know or what I can achieve — if I don't follow in Jesus' likeness all else is futile.

You may ask, how did you become aware? I don't know how —I just did. And that to me means that the Holy Spirit impressed it on my heart.

KEYWORDS: Rooted, Trust, Obey, Joy, Peace

SCRIPTURES

ROOTED
Colossians: 2:7 "**rooted** and built up in Him, and established in the faith, as you have been taught, abounding in it with thanksgiving." (NKJ)

Ephesians: 3: 16-17 "that He would grant you, according to the riches of His glory, to be strengthened with might through His Spirit in the inner man. That Christ may dwell in your hearts through faith; that you, being **rooted** and grounded in love, ... " (NKJ)

TRUST
Proverbs 3: 5-6 "Trust in the Lord with all your heart, and lean not on your own understanding; in all your ways acknowledge Him, and He shall direct your paths." (NKJ)

JOY
Psalm 4: 7 "You have put gladness in my heart, more than in the season that their grain and wine increased." (NKJ)

FOR FURTHER READING: **1 John 1**

OBEY
Acts 5: 27-29 "And when they had brought them they set them before the council. And the High Priest asked them, 'Did we not strictly command you not to teach in this name? And look, you filled Jerusalem with your doctrine, and intend to bring this man's blood on us.' But Peter and the other apostles answered, 'We ought to obey God rather than men'." (NKJ)

FURTHER READING

JOY
Nehemiah 8: 10

HOPE
Proverbs 10: 28

PRAYER SONG

SPIRIT WIND

You grace the world with beauty and love

On Your spirit wind comes the gentle dove

The perfumed flowers fill the air

With all of this You show how You care.

You gently lead on your Spirit wind

O Jesu joy of my desire

You lift my soul that I may find

The bounty of Your love, Sire.

How green are the trees in the summer haze

In the wild flower meadow I can only gaze

At each perfect colour and hue

That each year You create anew.

You gently lead on Your Spirit wind

O Jesu joy of my desire

You lift my soul that I may find

The bounty of Your love, Sire.

The wondrous hues of the mighty oceans

I stand enthralled at the mighty motion;

The surf on the waves gives a cresting of white

And gladdens my eyes — what a wonderful sight..

You gently lead on Your Spirit wind

O Jesu joy of my desire

You lift my soul that I may find

The bounty of Your love, Sire.

11th APRIL 2000

I was in that secret place again, so I put on my CD and hoped that I would meet with Jesus.

I closed my eyes and whispered, "Jesus". — There He was. Jesus started to climb a steep mountain. I followed, but had to stop at times to regain my strength. We were almost at the top, but there were some boulders to overcome. Jesus took me by the hand and gently pulled me up. As He did so my eyes fastened on the closest to perfect place I have ever seen. Mountains of purple and lilac, blue and a heather-mixture. In the midst of all this a sunset of the most vivid reds, yellows and oranges.

"Oh!" I breathed as I revelled in the sight. We sat down and surveyed the scene. After a while the Lord said, "Come, child, we must go." I felt joy and a peace spreading through the whole of my body.

INTERPRETATION

Where there is joy there is no fear, but where there is fear there is no joy. Whenever I "overdo it" in the workplace I naturally start to stumble and my work is not at its best because I am tired. Again Jesus made me realise that if I rest in Him I will experience joy and peace once more.

I started to look at those words, "Rest in Him".
Jesus said, "Come to me all you who are weary and burdened, and I will give you rest".
Rest in Jesus. Who is Jesus?
Jesus is the giver of life, the saver of souls, the Son of the Almighty Father – He is the Word become flesh!

So if Jesus is the Word become flesh then He wants us to rest in Him — the Word of God. There are many forms of rest but I felt in this particular walk that Jesus wanted me to rest in the Word of God. In Matthew 11: 28-30 the Lord calls us to walk in His ways and there we will find rest. It all starts to make sense. How can we know His ways unless we read the Word? The Lord has been impressing on me for some time to read more of His Word and in doing so I will find the key — and my soul will find rest.

KEY WORDS

Rest, Joy, Peace

SCRIPTURES

REST

Psalm 91:1
   He who dwells in the shelter of the most high
   Will rest in the shadow of the Almighty. (NKJ)

Matthew 11: 28-30 "Come to me all you who labour and are heavy laden, and I will give you rest. Take my yoke upon you and learn from Me, for I am gentle and lowly in heart and you will find rest for your souls. For My yoke is easy and My burden is light". (NKJ)

NIV Study Bible – *"Resting in Jesus is the absence of guilt, worry, anxiety and lack of meaning. Jesus promises meaning and hope, assurance, peace and joy even in the troubles we must endure in life."*

Resting in Jesus is the giving up of our guilt, worries, anxieties and fears and leaving them with Him. Sometimes we hold onto guilt and anxieties for many years because it is all we know and we feel comfortable with what we know, even though it could be harming us. The only way we can have full understanding of resting in Jesus is to read the Word. We cannot rest in Him if we don't know Him!

PRAYER SONG

RESTING IN YOU JESUS

I sit at Your feet
And there lies my peace
I gaze at your face
And behold Your grace.

*Resting in You Jesus
This is the key
Following You Lord
Helps me to see.*

I read Your Word Lord
and it penetrates deep.
It helps me move forward
Your commandments to keep.

*Resting in You Jesus
This is the key
Following you Lord
Helps me to be.*

13th APRIL 2000

I went to my 'secret place' and saw Jesus again.

"Hello Father," I said.
"Hello child," replied Jesus.
"Where are we going today Lord?" I asked.
Jesus replied, "You will see."

I put my hand in the hand of Jesus and skipped alongside Him (I had become as a child, with complete trust).
We went through a narrow rock passage. The opening became wider and suddenly in front of us was a large black pool. I looked

into the water and saw a glowing form. I knew this to be Jesus.

I felt warmth and protection coming from that glowing form. Others were looking into the pool although I couldn't make out their faces in the water. I looked down again and realised that I could not see my own reflection. I asked Jesus what did it mean? He replied, "You must trust Me child."

INTERPRETATION

When I don't quite understand what is happening around me, I must put my trust in the Lord. When things of darkness happen I must trust the Lord at all times. I must rebuke Satan and inform him that by the power invested in me, he has no authority in my life.

If people falsely accuse me or pretend to be what they are not, then my trust must be with the Lord. In Him is my protection and my shelter.

KEYWORDS
Father, Protection, Trust, Darkness

SCRIPTURES

FATHER
Isaiah 9: 6 And he will be called Wonderful Counsellor, Mighty God, Everlasting Father, Prince of Peace.

PROTECTION
John 17: 11 "I will remain in the world no longer, but they are still in the world, and I am coming to You. Holy Father, protect them by the power of Your name – the name You gave Me – so that they may be one as We are one."

TRUST
Psalm 32: 10 Many are the woes of the wicked, but the Lord's unfailing love surrounds the man who trusts in Him.

DARKNESS
Job 34: 22 There is no dark place, no deep shadow, where evildoers can hide.

2 Peter 1: 19 And we have the word of the prophets made more certain, and you will do well to pay attention to it, as to a light shining in a dark place. Until the day dawns and the morning star rises in your heart. (ST.R.B.)

PRAYER SONG

O SPIRIT OF JESUS

O Spirit of Jesus
Here is my heart
O Spirit of Jesus
Never to part.

O Spirit of Jesus
Show me the way
O Spirit of Jesus
Guide me each day.

O Spirit of Jesus
You're renewing my soul
O Spirit of Jesus
You are my goal.

When all your hopes are shattered, when people disappoint you, remember there is someone who will never disappoint you, someone who will love you to the very end – He is Jesus.
Taken from TRUST GOD by M. Basilea Schlink.

16ᵀᴴ APRIL 2000

"Hello Jesus," I said.
"Hello child, let us walk," Jesus replied.
All around me was a fog. I called out to Jesus, "Lord, I cannot see where I am going."
Jesus responded, "You are not meant to see. Let us sit while you rest in Me."
After a while the Lord said, "Come, walk with Me again."
I stumbled on a large stone in the road and nearly fell to the

ground, but Jesus' hand was there to steady me.

We walked on and came to a black door.

"What's behind the door, Jesus?" I enquired.

"Heaven," He replied.

"Can I go in Father?"

"No child, you are not ready."

I asked Jesus, "Why is the door so black?"

Jesus replied, "The world is full of darkness; come - I am the way, the truth and the life. I am the light that will guide you to My Father's place."

INTERPRETATION

What a walk! I could see that the black door was of the world. Sometimes we are in such a mess with our life, whether it is at our place of work or in the home and the fog is all around. Again I had to learn to rest in Jesus! I felt also that He was telling me that there was no other way but through Him, through His Word. The Word of God is the truth in all its essence. I wanted to know Jesus in a more intimate way, more so than I had ever wanted before and I knew that I must seek Him through His Word. The Lord has great patience with me.

The truth is the truth and lies are lies. I do not deceive myself that so-called white lies are acceptable; they are not; they are lies. A sin is a sin no matter how small it may appear. To God a sin is a sin. To move on spiritually I must recognise this truth. I realised that at that moment in time I was seeking the whole truth. There were areas in my life that were full of pretence, e.g. pretending everything was all right when, quite obviously, it wasn't.

KEYWORDS

The Word of God, Truth, Guidance, Life.

SCRIPTURES

LIGHT
2 Samuel 22: 29 For You are my lamp O Lord. The Lord shall enlighten my darkness. (NKJ)

Psalm 119: 105 Your Word is a lamp to my feet and a light to my path. (NKJ)

WORD OF GOD
Psalm 130: 5 I wait for the Lord, my soul waits, and in His Word I put my hope.

THE WAY, THE TRUTH, AND THE LIFE
John 14: 6 "I am the way, the truth and the life, no one comes to the Father except through me. "

PRAYER SONG

When I am weak Lord
It is you I must seek;
When on my own
With you I am grown.

Every day with Jesus
I want to be
Every day Jesus
Just You and me.

Your hand is guiding
Your love abiding
You show the way
Just every day.

Every day Jesus
I want to be
Every day Jesus
Just you and me.

I rely on you Lord
To see me through ;
You are my goal
You're in control.

17TH APRIL 2000

I met with Jesus and walked with Him, and gradually a feeling of wondrous joy filled my being. The love I felt for the Lord was deep.

I had been concerned for some time about how long I should continue to work on the thyroid project. The work I was involved in* was to raise awareness of misinterpretation and total reliance on thyroid blood test results. I asked the Lord how long did He want me to continue?
He replied, "Child, (Jesus always addressed me as "Child") there

will come a time when you must stop, but I will give you clear indication at that time."

"When will that be Jesus?" I enquired.

"Enough, child," *He replied gently.*

*See *'Tears Behind Closed Doors'* by Diana Holmes ISBN 0-9543106-0-8

INTERPRETATION

Two words, gently spoken, told me that it was not for me to know when I was to finish with the thyroid work. I knew I had been disciplined, but in the gentlest way. I reasoned with myself that if I knew everything that was to happen to me in my life there would be no growth. Jesus' will for my life would always be the best that there could be, although I was still given choice.

Sometimes I make the wrong choices and then have to endure the consequences; and that was when I grew in maturity. Growth doesn't come easy – it can be very painful.

KEYWORDS
Discipline, Choice, Maturity

SCRIPTURES

DISCIPLINE
Proverbs 3: 11 My son, do not despise the Lord's discipline, and do not resent His rebuke, because the Lord disciplines those He loves.

Proverbs 10: 17 He who heeds discipline shows the way to life, but whoever ignores correction leads others astray.

Proverbs 12: 1 "Whoever loves discipline loves knowledge, but he who hates correction is stupid."

Proverbs 15: 32 "He who ignores discipline despises himself, but whoever heeds correction gains understanding."

PRAYER SONG

DISCIPLINE

Please work in me Lord
A disciplined heart;
Help me become assured
Of Yours the loving way.

Please work in me Lord
An obedient soul
And teach me to recognise
Your will is my goal.

Please work in me Lord
A joyful heart
And let me step forward
with joy to impart.

Please work in me Lord
The child I could be
The child of Your heart
The child that You see.

18ᵀᴴ APRIL 2000

"Hello Father," I said almost in a whisper.

"Hello child," He replied gently.

"Where are we going today?" I asked.

"You will see."

We walked along a narrow road and suddenly we were in the clouds. It felt as though I was under a warm shower.

"Rest here and I will refresh you," said Jesus.

Many times Jesus did not speak, yet I knew what to do. Soon we were on our way again along the same narrow road. There was nothing to see on this road and I pointed this out to Jesus.

"This is the road of perseverance."

And then He said, "I will go ahead of you now." Suddenly He was gone!

I felt afraid; and then I saw a small light at the end of the road and felt spurred on. I stood up and walked on.

INTERPRETATION

Prior to this walk my thoughts had been on my marriage, which was suffering. Also thoughts were on the second edition of *Tears Behind Closed Doors*. I was using an old laptop, which was proving to be a nightmare. The amount of research I was involved in was quite overwhelming and I needed to wade through it very carefully. I knew that the Lord would help me in both of these areas.

I knew that the Lord was impressing on me to 'rest in Him' and then persevere with my work. I was researching the addition of fluorides into domestic water supplies. I had to sift through stacks of 'papers', extract what I wanted and then find a corresponding research paper to back up what I had found.

Set out below is a piece of information for the reader:

Fluoride was given in the 1930s – 1950s for people with an overactive thyroid gland to bring down the thyroid hormone levels. My question is: why are the authorities adding it to our water supplies?

KEYWORDS

Rest, perseverance

SCRIPTURES

REST
Psalm 91:1 He who dwells in the secret place of the Most High shall abide under the shadow of the Almighty.

PERSEVERANCE
Romans 5:3 Not only that, but we also glory in tribulations, knowing that tribulation produces perseverance, and perseverance character and character hope.

Hebrews 12:1 Therefore since we are surrounded by a great cloud of witnesses, let us throw off everything that hinders and the sin that so easily entangles, and let us run with perseverance the race marked out for us.

James 1:4 Perseverance must finish its work so that you may be mature and complete, and not lacking anything.

PRAYER SONG

TO BE STILL

Take me by the hand Lord,
Teach me to be still
To know that You are God
And when I'm in Your will.

Teach me how to pray Lord
Create a pure new heart
Teach me how to pray Lord
And then I'll do my part.

Show to me obedience
That I must give to You
Trusting in the confidence
It will make my life anew.
Show me perseverance
To continue on the way
To carry out the work for You
Without undue delay.

APRIL 20TH 2000

I walked with Jesus beside a riverbank where there were many trees alongside. The Lord walked down to the river edge and knelt down. He put His fingers in the water against the flow and remarked:
"See, the flow is interrupted and the power is lost. Do not let your relationship with Me be interrupted or your power will be lost."

INTERPRETATION

My relationship with Jesus must not be interrupted and I must not do things in my own strength, or my power in Jesus will be lost. Focus on Jesus and fellowship with Him is the only way to maturity.

I must endeavour to ignore the temptations that come my way, for they take me away from my quiet times with the Lord. It is easy to have something else to do and say to yourself: "I will have my quiet time later" – but later never comes. We all fall into this trap. The Word of the Lord is paramount to knowing Him and following Him.

KEYWORDS

Power, Strength, Temptation

SCRIPTURES

POWER
Acts 1:8 But you will receive power when the Holy Spirit comes on you; and you will be my witnesses in Jerusalem, and in all Judea and Samaria and to the ends of the earth.

STRENGTH
Exodus 15:2 The Lord is my strength and my song; He has become my salvation. He is my God

and I will praise Him, my father's God, and I will exalt Him.

TEMPTATION

Matthew 6:13 And do not lead us into temptation, but deliver us from the evil one. For Yours is the Kingdom and the power and the glory forever. (NKJ).

Matthew 26:41 Watch and pray lest you enter into temptation. The spirit is willing but the flesh is weak. (NKJ)

PRAYER SONG

SWEETEST LOVE

Sweet dreams of Jesus
In my waking hour
You tell of Your love Lord
And fill me with power.

Yours is the sweetest love
Your fragrance all around
I am lost in wonder
As Your love abounds.

Show me how to share Lord
Yours, this wondrous love,
So that I can tell all
It comes from heaven above.

21st APRIL 2000

Jesus walked, I skipped (I had become as a child).

"Let us sit here a while," said Jesus, pointing to a large rock. He went on to say, "Look to the spirit within, the spirit I gave to you, the spirit of love – and do not let any intrusion from elsewhere interfere with that spirit."

Jesus left me and I pondered on what He said.

INTERPRETATION

Jesus loved – that I knew. My spirit within, the spirit He gave me – that is what He said. Jesus is the spirit within; it is His spirit in me and Jesus is love. That inner voice gently telling me the right way. How many times had I heard the Spirit within me giving me guidance, only to brush it aside with my own intellect?

Dear Jesus – thank you for this walk, this revelation. I knew that I must make more of a conscious effort to heed the guidance of the Lord and bring my soul in line with Him.

God gave us the gift of love. Whether we give out that love is entirely up to us. We can show love in many ways. As a physical hug or a kiss or by the things we do for others. We can also give love consciously from our heart to the heart of another being by a thought process. By doing this it can have a powerful effect on the other person.

KEYWORDS

The Spirit, Love

SCRIPTURES

THE SPIRIT
Job 33:4 The Spirit of God has made me, and the breath of the Almighty gives me life. (NKJ)

LOVE
Galatians 5:22 But the fruit of the Spirit is love, joy, peace, patience, kindness, goodness, faithfulness, gentleness and self-control. Against such things there is no law.

I FELT GUIDED TO ADD:

'TESTING OF THE SPIRITS'

1 John 4:1 Dear friends, do not believe every spirit, but test the spirits to see whether they are from God, because many false prophets have gone out into the world.

This is how you can recognise the Spirit of God. Every spirit that acknowledges that Jesus Christ has come in the flesh is from God, but every spirit that does not acknowledge Jesus is not from God. This is the spirit of the Anti-Christ, which you have heard is coming and even now is already in the world.

PRAYER SONG

O DEAREST HEART

O dearest heart of my longing
You touch my soul O Lord
I'm like a flower burst into bloom
You awakened the spirit within.

The oil of Your grace
Feeds the flame of the work
That You began in me
You bless and teach me so tenderly
You invade my heart O Lord.

27TH APRIL 2000

The road was sandy and stony. Oh what comfort, there in the distance was Jesus. I ran to Him and slipped my hand in His. Soon we found a well-worn rock to sit on. Many people must have sat here before. We surveyed the scene before us, which was full of beauteous wonder.

The mountains were like gentle giants sweeping down to the sea. The latter was a deep turquoise. After a while Jesus said, "Let us walk." I stopped to look back and Jesus said, "Do not delay."

His words were like a warning to me. I must not linger too much on the past but go forward into the future.

We reached a vast open space. I became afraid because of its emptiness, and spoke to Jesus about this. His response was, "Your heart will never be empty when it is full of Me."

INTERPRETATION

Within our hearts is the Spirit of Jesus. If I fill my mind (soul) full of the Lord then it is true my heart will never be empty – no room for fear.

I must not linger on the past too much. If the past is hurtful then each visitation there will only bring with it pain. The Lord God is not in the past, He is in the present, and so is His will for me – in the present.

I can have beautiful memories and relive them, but still it is not healthy to dally too long, for I can't live on dreams. Jesus' Word is my daily bread, my food to carry me through this life with all its adversities. Jesus' Word is my sunshine and can soothe my body and soul and refresh me.

KEYWORDS

Past, Empty   The Word

SCRIPTURES

PAST
Isaiah 43: 18   "Forget the former things, do not dwell on the past."

EMPTY
1 Peter 1: 18   For you know that it was not with perishable things such as silver or gold that you were redeemed from the empty way of life handed down to you from your forefathers, but with the precious blood of Christ, a lamb without blemish or defect.

For further reading: **Isaiah 29: 8**

THE WORD
Psalm 119: 11   I have hidden Your Word in my heart that I might not sin against You.

PRAYER SONG

Fill me with Your Holy Spirit
Jesus Christ my Lord
Imprint upon my heart this day
The beauty of Your Word.

Fill me, Jesus, with Your love
That I may give it away
Send me angels from above
Today and every day.

Fill me with Your strength Lord
To see me through each day
Give me power too Lord
That I may stay on the way.

29th APRIL 2001

I was standing on my own, and suddenly there was Jesus, all light and love. I ran to Him. We climbed up a crag-ridden mountain path and reached a place where we sat for a while. Jesus said to me, "Rest, child, you are weary."

I wept. After a while we walked again and came upon young lambs suckling. When they finished they came to us and we gave them love.

We walked on and reached the top of the mountain. Jesus said,

"Keep resting in Me child and I will give you streams of living water to refresh you. You are my child and I love you. Do not be too busy in your work to spend time with Me."

INTERPRETATION

I weep, sometimes out of frustration, for all the people who suffer illness. Their despair is heartbreaking. I was in that situation myself in 1994. After 23 years of ill health, 6 misdiagnoses, and finally having to use a wheelchair, I was correctly diagnosed in 1994 with an underactive thyroid gland. I became well and since then I have been researching and raising awareness of the need for a change in clinical practice with regard to the interpretation and total reliance on thyroid blood test results. Sometimes I have exhausted myself in my endeavours, and the Lord was having a hard time getting through to me that I must "rest in Him". How patient is the Lord.

The Lord was also telling me to take time out with His creation to bring about a balance in my life.

KEYWORDS
Rest, Time, Water, Love, Tears

SCRIPTURES

TEARS
Revelation 7:17 For the Lamb at the centre of their throne will be their shepherd; He will lead them to springs of living water. And God will wipe away every tear from their eyes.

Psalm 126:5 Those who sow in tears will reap with songs of joy.

2 Chronicles 5:13 The trumpeters and singers joined in unison, as with one voice, to give praise and thanks to the Lord. Accompanied by trumpets, cymbals and other instruments, they raised their voices in praise to the Lord and sang: "He is good; His love endures forever."

WATER
John 4:14 "But whoever drinks the water I give him will never thirst. Indeed, the water I give him will become in him a spring of water welling up to eternal life."

John 7:38 "Whoever believes in Me, as the scripture has said, streams of living water shall flow from within him."

TIME
Luke 10:41-42 And Jesus answered and said unto her, "Martha, Martha thou art careful and troubled about many things: But one thing is needful: and Mary has chosen that good part, which shall not be taken away from her." (ST. R.B.)

PRAYER SONG

You lead me to the springs of life
O shepherd of the hills
And take away all my strife
Just as the Father wills.

You give Your love to me
O shepherd of the hills
You bid me take some time to be
Just as the Father wills.

I will never find one such as You
O shepherd of the hills
You offer to me eternity too
Just as the Father wills.

PRAYER

*Let me not live a life that's free
From the things that draw me close to Thee
For how can I ever hope to heal
The wounds of others I do not feel
If my eyes are dry and I never weep
How do I know when the hurt is deep?
If my heart is cold and it never bleeds
How can I tell what my brother needs?
For when ears are deaf to the beggar's plea
And we close our eyes and refuse to see
And we steel our hearts and harden our minds
And we count it a weakness whenever we're kind
We're no longer following the Father's way
Or seeking His guidance from day to day
So spare me no heartache or sorrow, dear Lord
For the heart that hurts reaps the biggest reward*

*And God blesses the heart that is broken with sorrow
As He opens the door for a brighter tomorrow —
For only through tears can we recognise
The suffering that lies in another's eyes.*

(SOURCE UNKNOWN)

7TH MAY 2000

Jesus came and we walked. Suddenly Jesus' pace quickened. He was way ahead of me; so much that I had to run to catch up. And when I did Jesus said, "Concentrate, child."

We continued to walk for a while and then rested. I told Jesus of my love for Him.
"That is right, child."
His response seemed strange but full of love.

There was a light summer breeze and along the wayside were fragrant lilies. We came upon a blue sea, which sparkled like gems dancing in the sunlight. My whole being was full of love and enchantment in the Lord.

KEYWORDS

Love

INTERPRETATION

To love Jesus in fullness is to read the Word of God daily and live it out. To obey the commands of the Lord and share Jesus with others. Jesus wants to be loved actively not just verbally.

SCRIPTURES

LOVE
Psalm 57:9-10 "I will praise You O Lord, among the nations; I will sing of You among the peoples. For great is Your Love, reaching to the heavens; Your faithfulness reaches to the skies."

PRAYER SONG

Thank you Father for Your love
That You have sent from heaven above
You have covered me with a mantle of grace
That I may catch a glimpse of Your face.

You knew me before I was in the womb
And now You go to prepare a room
Thank You Father for choosing me
For Your grace and Word have set me free.

9th MAY 2000

In my vision I was a child, and then I became an adult again. I looked for Jesus; He was nowhere to be seen. I was not concerned because I knew He would come. There He was!

Our bodies lifted off the ground and the next thing I knew we were viewing the world. It was very strange; instead of blues and greens the colours were mostly black and red with a smattering of a white light here and there.

"What does it mean?" I enquired of Jesus.

Jesus' reply was quite chilling!

"The black denotes evil, the red — my children who are lost and in

pain. The white lights are those who are born again into the Spirit."
Just as suddenly we were walking on the ground again.

INTERPRETATION

This indeed was a disturbing walk! So many of the Lord's children in need of help. So much work to do. I know one thing — I must not rush out in my own strength and start doing things. If these walks with Jesus have taught me anything then it is to be guided by the Lord. I had a strong feeling that this walk was for the future and the Lord was just preparing me.

All those who are 'born again into the Spirit' have a responsibility to show those who are lost in the fog of ignorance the way to Jesus. I knew that the thyroid project was only a precursor of the work that I would be engaged in, in the future.

KEYWORDS

Evil, Lost, 'Born again'

SCRIPTURES

EVIL

Proverbs 10: 23 "A fool finds pleasure in evil conduct, but a man of understanding delights in wisdom."

Proverbs 11: 27 "He who seeks good finds goodwill, but evil comes to him who searches for it."

Proverbs 24: 20 "For the evil man has no future hope, and the lamp of the wicked will be snuffed out."

BORN AGAIN

John 3: 7 "You should not be surprised at my saying, 'You must be born again'."

1 Peter 1: 23 For you have been 'born again', not of perishable seed but of imperishable, through the living and enduring Word of God.

LOST

Luke 15: 6-7 "Then he calls his friends and neighbours together and says, 'Rejoice with me; I have found my lost sheep.' I tell you that in the same way there will be more rejoicing in heaven over one sinner who repents than over ninety-nine righteous persons who do not need to repent."

PRAYER SONG

Since I've been 'born again' in You
You've taught me how to live anew
    Myself You say I have to lose
    And tell others about the news.

*   CHORUS*
This side of Jesus
My wonderful Lord
This side of Jesus
Divine Counsellor

When Israel has come to You
And all have been chosen by Your grace
    You will no longer have to woo
    Surely then shall we see Your face.

This side of Jesus
My wonderful Lord
This side of Jesus
Divine Counsellor

I pray the day the rapture comes
    That I'll be prepared my Lord
I pray the day the rapture comes
    That I will not be flawed.

11th MAY 2000

"Hello Jesus," I said.
Jesus answered, "Child," in the gentlest voice.
That greeting in all its simplicity made me feel very special. His tone told me that He loved me and that He was expecting me.

Then in my vision we were astride donkeys in the desert. Jesus in front on a dark-coloured one and me behind on a lighter-coloured one. Without warning the wind blew up and the sand bit hard into my face, so that I had to keep my eyes tight shut. The wind dropped as suddenly as it had begun. Jesus was still in *front riding on His donkey and I had come to no harm. The wind came again many times and just as quickly abated.*

After what seemed an eternity we reached an oasis where there were fruit trees, water, shade and no wind. We stopped and rested and Jesus said to me,

"I will always carry you through adversity."

INTERPRETATION

This walk in its entirety told me in no uncertain terms that the Lord loved me unconditionally. With this walk I started to understand unconditional love.

More and more my focus must be on Jesus.

I wasn't foolish enough to believe that from now on everything would be 'plain sailing' but I knew that if I kept close to the Lord, He would uphold me in any battle. I also felt that this walk was a warning of tough times ahead

Over the next few years I would remember this particular walk.

KEYWORDS

Faith, Carry

SCRIPTURES

FAITH
2 Corinthians 5: 7 We live by faith, not by sight.

Hebrews 11: 1 Now faith is being sure of what we hope for and certain of what we do not see.

CARRY
Exodus 19: 4 "You yourselves have seen what I did to Egypt, and how I carried you on eagles' wings and brought you to Myself."

PRAYER SONG

FAITH

Bless me with faith O Jesus dear
To walk each day with You
With You in control and always near
My path is straight and true.

To have faith that You will carry me
Must always be my goal
Through all of life's adversity
This will bless my soul.

ATTITUDE

*I woke up early today, excited over all I get to do
Before the clock strikes midnight.
I have responsibilities to fulfil today
My job is to choose what kind of day
I am going to have.*

*Today I can complain
Because the weather is rainy
Or I can be thankful that the grass
is being watered for free.*

*Today I can feel sad
Because I don't have more money or
I can be grateful
For the many things that I already have.*

*Today I can grumble about my health
Or I can rejoice that I am alive
Today I can cry because roses have thorns
Or I can celebrate that thorns have roses.*

*Today I can mourn for my lack of friends
Or I can excitedly embark on a new quest
To discover new relationships.
Today I can whine because I have to go to work
Or I can shout for joy because I have a job to go to.*

*Today I can murmur dejectedly
Because I have to do the housework
Or I can feel honoured because the Lord has provided
Shelter for my mind body and soul.*

*What today will be like is up to me
I'm the one who gets to choose
What kind of day I will have.*

(AMERICAN AUTHOR UNKNOWN)

12TH MAY 2000

I met with Jesus and we walked and then rested. Jesus knew that I was troubled with the task ahead of me.
He said, "Remember the road of perseverance." I replied, "Yes Father, I do."
Jesus looked up and a white dove appeared. It landed on His

shoulder. He gently picked up the dove and placed it on my shoulder and said, "There, my peace I give you, go in peace and complete your task."

INTERPRETATION

Every time I walked with Jesus there was a time of rest. I knew that Jesus was communicating to me that I must have fellowship with Him. To do this I must study His word so that it is ingrained on my very soul. The illustration of the dove was to let me know that there would be peace after every fellowship with Him; the dove being a symbol of the Holy Spirit.

KEYWORDS

Fellowship, Peace

SCRIPTURES

FELLOWSHIP
2 Corinthians 13:14 May the grace of the Lord Jesus Christ, and the love of God, and the

fellowship of the Holy Spirit be with you all.

PEACE
Colossians 3:15
Let the peace of Christ rule in your heart, since as members of one body you were called to peace. And be thankful. (ST.R.B.)

PRAYER SONG

THE WORD

I praise Your holy name
Jesus Christ my Lord
I am so glad you came
Into my life with Your Word.

You are life itself to me
For me there is no other
You came so that I may see
You are to me my lover.

Your guiding hand always there
Your gentleness unspoken
Healing all of the wounds
When my body is broken.

Your peace You give to me
When I call out Your name
My friend You ever will be
Jesus You are the same
Thank you Lord Jesus.

20th MAY 2000

Jesus was waiting for me. He beckoned and said, "Come."

"Where are we going, Jesus?" I enquired.

"I will show you the way," He replied.

We reached a beautiful leafy glade by the sea, where sunlight streamed through the trees and alighted on the water, skipping over the waves and turning the sea into a myriad of the tiniest jewels.

We sat down on nearby rocks. A tiny bird flew onto Jesus' shoulder and sang to Him. Animals started appearing through the trees.

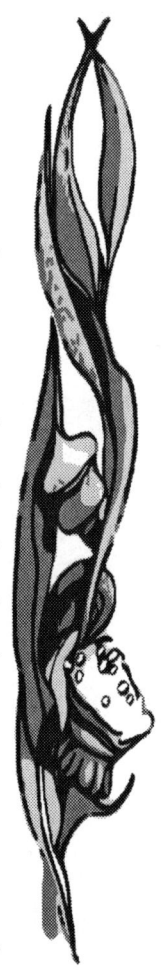

A young deer came and placed its head on Jesus' lap, looking up at Him with love, and then suddenly scampered off. This happened many times with different animals and birds. The place was full of love.

INTERPRETATION

The love that the birds and animals gave to Jesus was a sight to behold. There was trust in their eyes. As a child I had always trusted and even into early womanhood, but for many years now I have found it difficult to trust people. Jesus was teaching me trust and unconditional love. I had to change my mindset.

To come away from being on the defensive and instead to pour out unconditional love was going to be quite a challenge and I knew that it was not going to happen overnight.

KEYWORDS
Love, Trust, Strength

SCRIPTURES

LOVE
1 Corinthians 13: 4 Love is patient, Love is kind. It does not envy, it does not boast, it is not proud. Love does not delight in evil but rejoices with the truth.

TRUST
Psalm 56: 4 In God whose word I praise, in God I trust; I will not be afraid. What can mortal man do to me?

STRENGTH
Philippians 4: 13 I can do everything through Him who gives me strength.

PRAYER SONG

Holiest of Holies
You are the way
The freedom that You gave us
Is ours today.

Jesus the way of life
We must follow Him
He will see us through all strife
He died to forgive our sin.

Jesus You're all majesty
Glory personified
I bow my head before You
And pray that self has died.

CHORUS

26TH MAY 2000

"Come with Me child," said Jesus. I followed Him and suddenly a storm came upon us. I ran to Jesus, He held open His cloak and wrapped it around me and said, "You are safe. I will let no harm come to you."
The storm abated and Jesus said, "See, all is well."

INTERPRETATION
I see now that through all times of adversity Jesus has protected me. Many times I would have run away from an adverse situation, but now, by the grace of God, I stay with and through these situations. There are times when we have to move away from adversity, but that in itself can be a moving on.

KEYWORDS

Protection, Grace

SCRIPTURES

PROTECTION
Psalm 32: 7 You are my hiding place; You will protect me from trouble and surround me with songs of deliverance.

2 Peter 3: 18 But grow in the grace and knowledge of our Lord and Saviour Jesus Christ. To Him be glory both now and for ever! Amen.

Hebrews 4: 16 Let us then approach the throne of grace with confidence, so that we may receive mercy and find grace to help us in our time of need.

PRAYER SONG

WONDERFUL SAVIOUR

O wonderful Saviour
O wonderful Lord
Your grace I need
In word and deed.

O wonderful Saviour
O wonderful Lord
You pour on me blessings
And then I'm restored.

O wonderful Saviour
O wonderful Lord
You show me Your love
In that I'm secured.

30TH MAY 2000

I followed Jesus along a path in a dense wood. To our right there was a narrow river flowing. The water was clear, and as it rippled over the stones the water was transformed into soft foam. Further ahead was a bridge. We walked onto it and watched the water wend its way downstream. It was very peaceful. The stillness was broken by Jesus' gentle voice saying, "What is happening to the water?"

I looked hard but did not understand for a time, but after a while I said, "It is flowing forward."

Jesus spoke again: "That is what you must do; flowing water never turns back on itself. Go forward to your future. Come, child."

We moved away from the bridge and I followed Him through a dense thicket, which opened out onto a garden of paradise.

INTERPRETATION

The Lord was telling me not to dwell on the past. The past was gone – I had to go forward into the future with boldness. The water in the river flows forward boldly; if it didn't it would never reach its destination.

If I stop on the way to the future then I will miss something that the Lord has in mind, and it will take longer to fulfil the plan that He has for my life. Or if I dally too long He could choose someone else.

KEYWORD

Path

SCRIPTURES

PATH

Proverbs 3: 6 In all your ways acknowledge Him, and He will make your paths straight.

Psalm 25: 4 Show me your ways O Lord, teach me Your paths.

FOR FURTHER READING

Isaiah 26: 7
Psalm 27: 11

PRAYER SONG

O SWEET FACE OF JESUS

O sweet face of Jesus if I could see
With longing held so dear
Your further guidance for my path
That I might not shed these tears.

Forgive me Lord if I find it hard
To follow the path of Your choosing
Mistakes I make along the way
That I am afraid of losing.

But You have shown to me Your truth
In this I should do Your work
I pray that my attitude be Your will
And Your love will be my walk.

4ᵀᴴ JUNE 2000

I saw Jesus and went to Him.
"Jesus I love You; may I walk with You?" I said.
"Yes child," Jesus replied.
A white dove came into view and flew straight on to the back of Jesus' hand. The dove was pure white like the driven snow.
"Trust and obey," said Jesus, and with that the dove flew off.

I had pressing issues that I needed to ask Jesus about. Should I include the fluoride issue at the next meeting with the Department of Health? He replied, "My Spirit will tell you what to do, come, rest in Me."

INTERPRETATION

Jesus was teaching me to seek His Spirit and so didn't answer me directly. I was to spend time with the Holy Spirit and He would give guidance through the Word.

KEYWORDS

Trust, Obey, Truth

TRUST
Proverbs 3: 5-6 Trust in the Lord with all thine heart and lean not on thine own understanding. (ST.R.B.)
Psalm 71: 1 In Thee, O Lord, do I put my trust: let me never be put to confusion. (ST. R. B.)
Psalm 32: 10 Many are the woes of the wicked, But the Lord's unfailing love surrounds the man who trusts in Him.
Psalm 56: 4 In God, whose Word I praise, in God I trust. I will not be afraid. What can mortal man do to me?
OBEY
John 14: 23 Jesus answered and said to him. "If anyone loves Me, he will keep My Word; My Father will love him and we will come to him and make our home with him." (NKJ)

Deuteronomy 13: 4 "You shall walk after the Lord Your God and fear Him, and keep His commandments and obey His voice; you shall serve Him and hold fast to Him." (NKJ)
Acts 5: 29 Then Peter and the other apostles answered and said, "We ought to obey God rather than men." (ST.R.B.)

TRUTH
John 16: 13 "However, when He, the Spirit of truth, has come, He will guide you into all truth; for He will not speak on His own authority, but whatever He hears He will speak; and He will tell you of things to come." (NKJ)

FOR FURTHER READING

Deuteronomy 6:3

PRAYER SONG

HOLY SPIRIT OF JESUS CHRIST MY FATHER

Spirit of Jesus rest in me

Open my eyes and let me see

That for You to be in control

Should always be my goal.

Chorus:

Holy Spirit of Jesus Christ

My Father Three In One

You are everything to me

Thank You for all You have done.

I need You now O Jesus please

For You are my strength; You hold the key

When I am weak You are strong

O dear Lord Jesus to You I belong.

Holy Spirit of Jesus Christ

My Father Three In One

You are everything to me

Thank You for all You have done.

Dear Lord Jesus You give me choice

But now I pray that I hear Your voice

To do Your will is what I must heed

In every word and every deed.

Holy Spirit of Jesus Christ

My Father Three In One

You are everything to me

Thank You for all You have done.

23rd JUNE 2000

I walked with Jesus. The birds were flying high in the sky. I loved the birds!
Jesus took me through some very dense, lush green grasses. We entered a clearing in the wood. I looked down into a pool of water. Suddenly the pool became all light, and no water was showing at all. Just light.
Jesus said, "I am the light of the world; bathe in this and you will be refreshed."

INTERPRETATION

Another reminder from Jesus that He is the Word made flesh and that I must soak myself in the Scriptures and in turn I will be refreshed.

KEYWORD

Light

SCRIPTURES

LIGHT

John 8: 12 When Jesus spoke again to the people, He said, "I am the light of the world. Whoever follows Me will never walk in darkness, but will have the light of life."

Psalm 27: 1 The Lord is my light and my salvation — whom shall I fear? The Lord is the stronghold of my life — of whom shall I be afraid?

FOR FURTHER READING

Isaiah 2: 5
Psalm 56: 13

PRAYER SONG

THREE IN ONE

I praise Your Holy name
Your light is shining so
Three In One you are the same
You show the way to go.

I praise Your Holy name
Your Spirit dwells in me
Three In One You are the same
Following You helps me to see.

24th JUNE 2000

There was Jesus. We walked and arrived at the water's edge of a large lake. Jesus bent down and picked up three stones. One was irregular, one was pitted, and one was smooth. Jesus showed them to me. I enquired of Him, "What does it mean?"

Jesus proceeded to tell me. "The irregular stone: the inconsistent, the pitted one is flawed, and the smooth one is bound in Me."

There was a short silence; then Jesus said, "You are in the world but not of it. Go and tell the people of My love."

INTERPRETATION

Jesus was warning me about certain types of people.

IRREGULAR STONE – This stone represented a person who is inconsistent and with no strength of character. One who sits on the fence. A person who likes to party in both camps, and therefore will sit with both and agree with both, thus one with no principles. In effect this person has lost their integrity. On the outside this person appears to be righteous but they are full of hypocrisy.

PITTED STONE – This stone represented a person who has a flaw in their character. Someone not to be trusted — a gossip or someone who is a troublemaker. It could be a person whose life is in total disorder but believes that everybody else is wrong except them. These people are hypocritical and critical.

SMOOTH STONE – This stone represented someone who is bound up in love, which is: The Way, the Truth and the Life — in essence: Jesus — the Word.

KEYWORDS

Hypocrisy, Gossip, Love

SCRIPTURES

HYPOCRISY
Matthew 23: 28 "In the same way on the outside you appear to people as righteous but on the inside you are full of hypocrisy and wickedness."
Psalm 26: 4 I do not sit with deceitful men, nor do I consort with hypocrites.

GOSSIP
Proverbs 16: 28 A perverse man stirs up dissension and a gossip separates close friends.

LOVE
1 John 4: 16 And so we know and rely on the love God has for us. God is LOVE. Whoever lives in Love lives in God, and God in him.
1 John 3: 1 How great is the love the Father has lavished on us that we should be called the children of God! And that is what we are! The reason the world does not know us is that it did not know Him.

FURTHER READING

TALEBEARER
Proverbs 26: 20
HYPOCRISY
1 Peter 2: 1
LOVE
Romans 5: 5; 1 John 4

PRAYER SONG

GENTLE SPIRIT OF JESUS' LOVE

The gentle Spirit of Jesus' love
Fills me with radiance from above
That I may receive His power
That He promised me in that final hour.

Chorus:
Spirit of Jesus
Please change my heart
Spirit of Jesus
I'll do my part
Create in me anew
A person that's just like You.

The unconditional depth of Your love
Brings me to shame when I fail to move
To spread the word about Your grace
So that people may choose to seek Your face.

Spirit of Jesus
Please change my heart
Spirit of Jesus
I'll do my part
Create in me anew
A person that's just like You.

You've taught me patience and tolerance
Forgive me Lord when it doesn't quite work
I must go out in faith and be good
And heed all the time Your precious Word.

Spirit of Jesus please change my heart
Spirit of Jesus
I'll do my part
Create in me anew
A person that's just like You.

23rd JULY 2000

I went to the 'secret place' and prayed to Jesus. I had overdone it. I walked until I found Jesus. He was sitting on a rock at the top of the mountain I had just climbed.
Jesus spoke: "See all this," pointing to the scene below, "this is the world; you are not of the world though you live in it. Heed the Word of God. Many times you will be tempted. You must say no to temptation."
There was a pause, then Jesus said, "Come." We walked in companionable silence.

INTERPRETATION

Once again the Lord was telling me that I was set apart from the world and I must come away from 'self' (the old me) and if I kept to His Word I would not be tempted to slip back into my old ways. As I said in describing the walk, I knew that I had overdone it. Sometimes we can give too much to people and they can and will drain us. I had to learn to say "No".

Becoming a new person in Christ is a process. In the first place you have to give your life to Jesus and repent of your sins, and that means coming away from sins past and present. You also have to believe that Jesus Christ died for your sins and redeemed you to give you the gift of eternal life with Him. If you have done that then your spirit is a new creation in Christ in an instant. Yes, Jesus is in you. Your soul, which is your mind, takes much longer to become changed. Years of pruning are ahead and sometimes it is very painful, because the 'nice person' that you thought you were doesn't really exist. Are you bristling yet! I did when I realised. We all have skeletons in the cupboard and the Lord wants them all destroyed. The Lord has forgiven us but we have to learn to forgive ourselves.

KEYWORDS

The world, the Word, Temptation

SCRIPTURES

THE WORLD
John 15: 19 "If you belonged to the world, it would love you as its own. As it is, you do not belong to the world, but I have chosen you out of the world. That is why the world hates you. "

THE WORD OF GOD
Hebrews 4: 12-13 For the Word of God is living and active. Sharper than any double-edged sword, it penetrates even to dividing soul and spirit, joints and marrow; it judges the thoughts and attitudes of the heart. Nothing in all creation is hidden from God's sight. Everything is uncovered and laid bare before the eyes of Him to whom we must give account.
James 1: 22-25 Do not merely listen to the Word, and so deceive yourselves. Do what it says. Anyone who listens to the Word but does not do what it says is like a man who looks at his face in the mirror, and after looking at himself, goes away and immediately forgets what he looks like. But the man who looks intently into the perfect law that gives freedom, and continues to do this, not forgetting what he has heard, but doing it — he will be blessed in what he does.

TEMPTATION
Matthew 26: 41 "Watch and pray so that you will not fall into temptation. The spirit is willing but the body is weak."

FURTHER READING:
TEMPTATION
Matthew 6: 13
THE WORLD
2 Corinthians 10: 3
THE WORD
Ephesians 6: 17

PRAYER SONG

IT COMES WITH JESUS' LOVE

When I am tempted I see Your Word
O Father God above
Sharper than any double-edged sword
It comes with Jesus' love.

When in the world but not of it
O Father God above
I see Your Holy Spirit descending
In the shape of a dove.

> Your Word is water to my soul
> O Father God above
> It cleanses and refreshes me
> And it comes with Jesus' love.

8ᵀᴴ AUGUST 2000

I met with Jesus at the edge of a field, which was full of beautiful wild flowers of yellow, red, orange, purple, white, pink, and blue — and I delighted in them. The stems were longer than I had ever seen before, so much so that I could barely see over the tops.

We came across a grassy bank with a gentle stream below. Jesus sat on the bank and I sat at His feet. We listened to the running water for a while.

After what seemed like hours Jesus said, "Rest."

INTERPRETATION

Again Jesus was reminding me, in yet another walk, to rest in Him. I was not to lose sight of Him and impressed on me was the feeling that there were hard times ahead. The amazing thing is that Jesus was telling me He would be with me. I felt greatly comforted by this.

When I am out with nature, for me it is easy to feel at peace, and Jesus was telling me that I must do this more often. (A year later I decided to get a little dog, so I went to the dogs' home and chose a little Yorkie-cross and named her Miss Muffy. I now go walking every day and take time out to be with nature, which is part of God's creation.)

KEYWORDS
Flowers, Water, Rest

SCRIPTURES
FLOWERS
Song of Solomon 2: 12:
"The flowers appear on the earth;
The time of singing has come,
And the voice of the turtledove
Is heard in our land." (NKJ)

WATER
Revelation 21: 6 He said to me: "It is done. I am the Alpha and the Omega, the Beginning and the End. To him who is thirsty I will give to drink without cost from the spring of the water of life".

REST   **Psalm 91:**
He who dwells in the shelter of the Most High
Will rest in the shadow of the Almighty.
I will say of the Lord, He is my refuge and my fortress,
My God, in whom I trust.
Surely He will save you from the fowler's snare
and from the deadly pestilence.
He will cover you with His feathers
and under His wings you will find refuge;
His faithfulness will be your shield and rampart.
You will not fear the terror of the night,
Nor the arrow that flies by day,
Nor the pestilence that stalks in the darkness,
Nor the plague that destroys at midday.
A thousand may fall at your side,
ten thousand at your right hand,
but it will not come near you.
You will only observe with your eyes
And see the punishment of the wicked.

If you make the Most High your dwelling —
Even the Lord, who is my refuge —
Then no harm will befall you,
No disaster will come near your tent.

> For He will command His angels concerning you
> To guard you in all your ways;
> They will lift you up in their hands,
> So that you will not strike your foot against a stone.
> You will tread upon the lion and the cobra;
> You will trample the great lion and the serpent.
> "Because he loves Me," says the Lord,
> "I will rescue him;
> I will protect him, for he acknowledges My name.
> He will call upon Me, and I will answer him;
> I will be with him in trouble,
> I will deliver him and honour him.
> With long life will I satisfy him
> and show him my salvation."

Jeremiah 6: 16 This is what the Lord says: "Stand at the crossroads and look; ask for the ancient paths, ask where the good way is, and walk in it, and you will find rest for your souls."

Matthew 11: 28-29 "Come to Me, all you who are weary and burdened, and I will give you rest. Take my yoke upon you and learn from Me, for I am gentle and humble in heart, and you will find rest for your souls. For My yoke is easy and My burden is light."

To me, Jesus is saying that although we will still have trials and tribulations in this life, if we stay close to His Word it will give our lives meaning, hope and peace.

FURTHER READING

WATER
Isaiah 49: 10

PRAYER SONG

WELLSPRING

You are the wellspring of my life
O Jesus Lord of all
You came and gently took me in
So that I should not fall.

You bade me rest in your Word
O Jesus Lord on high
That I should know the righteous way
Whenever trials are nigh.

10th AUGUST 2000

There was Jesus. He held out His hand to me; I gave Him mine. We walked in what seemed to be a darkened hole.

After a while we came to a flat area and in the centre was a crater. Jesus was urging me forward to the edge of the crater. I was afraid.

"Do not be afraid, child," Jesus said. I was reluctant to move forward but I put my faith in Jesus and walked to the edge. Jesus said, "Look down." Now I really was afraid. I felt the pressure of Jesus' hand in mine and stood transfixed for some minutes, then I moved forward and looked down.

"What do you see?" enquired Jesus.

"Nothing," I replied.

Jesus remarked, "Nothing is right, child. There is nothing to be afraid of."

INTERPRETATION

What a powerful message in this walk! Most of what we fear is in our imaginings. The crater, as I thought, should have been full of molten lava, but when I looked over the edge, I saw nothing. It was a shock, because I really believed that molten lava was what I was about to see. How many times do we conjure up in our mind's eye what in reality is not there at all. I did not feel for one moment that Jesus was telling me to look over the edge of every crater; He was just warning me not to make mountains out of molehills.

SCRIPTURES
FEAR

1 John 4: 18 There is no fear in love. But perfect love drives out fear, because fear has to do with punishment. The one who fears is not made perfect in love.

Isaiah 41: 10 So do not fear, for I am with you; do not be dismayed, for I am your God. I will strengthen you and help you; I will uphold you with My righteous right hand.

NELSON MANDELA:

Our greatest fear is not that we are inadequate.
Our deepest fear is that we are powerful beyond measure.
It is our light, not our darkness that most frightens us.
We ask ourselves – who am I to be brilliant, gorgeous,
talented, or fabulous?
Actually, who are you not to be?
Your playing small does not serve the world.

There is nothing enlightening about shrinking so far
That other people won't feel secure around you.
We are born to make manifest the glory that is within us.
It is not just in some of us, it is in everyone.
And as we let our light shine,
We unconsciously give others permission to do the same.
As we are liberated from our own fear, our presence
Automatically liberates others.

PRAYER SONG

FEAR

You teach me Lord
That I need not fear
But give all my concerns to You
You teach me Lord
That You can bear
All of my sorrows too.

You teach me Lord
Where there is fear
There can be no love
You teach me Lord
That I must hear
All that comes from heaven above.

You teach me Lord
That out of darkness
You will bring the light
You teach me Lord
When in the brightness
You will show Your might.

FOR FURTHER READING

Psalm 23: 4
Psalm 27: 1

13th August 2000

As we walked, the road became very dusty and stony. At the wayside there were bright flowers of yellow and purple. Jesus turned off the dusty road and began to walk down an embankment of rich green grass. I followed Him. We came over the rise and I marvelled at the sight before me. There, nestling in the valley, was the prettiest village. The cottage-type dwellings had red roofs and white walls and they lay in a valley of green. The whole picture was breathtaking.

As the sun went to sleep she lent her colours of red, orange and yellow to that beautiful scene. Jesus said, "All is not as it seems. There are many forms of good and evil down there, but first comes goodness; because goodness comes from the Lord — and then comes evil."

INTERPRETATION

I believed that the Lord was warning me, yet again, to be wary of certain people who appear to be friendly at first and then turn. They suck you in and when you are feeling comfortable they spit you out! When these situations have arisen before I have always had prior warning but I ignored it and paid for the consequences. I am wiser now.

KEYWORDS

Good, Beauty, Trust, Warning, Evil

SCRIPTURES

GOOD, EVIL

Psalm 34: 8 Taste and see that the Lord is good; blessed is the man who takes refuge in Him.

Psalm 86: 5 You are forgiving and good, O Lord, abounding in love to all who call to You.

Psalm 119: 68 You are good and what You do is good; teach me Your decrees.

PRAYER

Dear Lord Jesus, I pray for those who find it hard
to be kind to people. Are they
hurting? You know where they are.
Lord I pray for their minds to be clear of things hurtful in the past
and things hurtful in the present.
Amen

AUGUST 19TH 2000

It is a long wait today. I am tempted to walk, but the Holy Spirit impresses on me that I must wait. Suddenly Jesus appeared from behind a tree and beckoned me. "Come," He said.

I made my way towards the tree and realised that to get to where Jesus was I would have to go through brambles. By the time I got to Jesus I was badly cut all over. I fell on my knees in front of Him. Jesus laid His hands on my head and said, "The glory is to come." Then He left me.

INTERPRETATION

I was going through trials and tribulations in my personal life and I felt strongly that with perseverance everything would be worked out with the plan that God has for me and then the glory will follow. Thank You Jesus

KEYWORDS

Glory, Temptation, Trials and Tribulations

SCRIPTURES

TEMPTATION
Matthew 6: 13 And lead us not into temptation, but deliver us from the evil one.

TRIALS AND TRIBULATIONS
James 1: 2 Consider it pure joy, my brothers, whenever you face trials of many kinds, because you know that the testing of your faith develops perseverance. Perseverance must finish its work so that you may be mature and complete, not lacking anything.
Mark 8: 38 "If anyone is ashamed of Me and My words in this adulterous and sinful generation, the Son of Man will be ashamed of him when He comes in His Father's glory with the holy angels."

ADVERSITY

When I go through adversity
You teach me Lord to trust in Thee.
Faith I must have at every turn
I long for this so that I may learn.

I will meet each day anew
With perseverance to see me through
The key to all of this must be
Keep faith in Jesus — only then will I see.

27th AUGUST 2000

There was Jesus. "Come," He said. We walked down a mountainside that was covered with yellow buttercups. Further along we stepped onto a track and I could hear the sound of the ground crunching under our feet as we walked.

I slipped my hand into Jesus' hand and immediately felt His strength. We came to a bay of oceanic blues and greens. There was a lone boat, with a white sail, on the water. As we neared the water's edge the boat sailed toward us. Once moored, Jesus helped me into the boat, and we set sail.

The first part of the journey was calm and serene, then without warning a *wind came up that rocked the boat alarmingly. A storm followed, which was wreaking havoc on our small boat. Ropes came loose, fish baskets careered across the deck as the wind and rain mercilessly took their toll. Jesus said, "Trust in Me alone." Then it became calm again. The same thing happened several times. We headed back to the shore and Jesus helped me onto the quay.*

INTERPRETATION

Whatever adversities come my way I must trust in the Lord and Him alone. I was going through some distressing problems in my personal life.

I had started researching for the second edition of my book *Tears Behind Closed Doors* and so I was under a lot of stress.

An American publisher had promised to publish the Second Edition, and indeed had been in receipt of a copy of the manuscript for ten months, and then had let me down, stating that there were people who would not back me.

I had already had a lot of flak from various groups in the past and now it was coming to haunt me again. I felt sure that it was the same groups that had communicated with the publishers.

The Lord has brought me through so much in the past that my only wish in all of this is to trust in Him. If I abide in Him, He will not fail me.

KEYWORDS

Trust, Despair, Hopelessness

SCRIPTURES

TRUST

Psalm 56: 4-5 In God whose word I praise. In God I trust; I will not be afraid. What can mortal man do to me? All day long they twist my words; they are always plotting to harm me.

Proverbs 3: 5-6 Trust in the Lord with all your heart and lean not on your own understanding; in all your ways acknowledge Him and He will make your paths straight.

John 14: 1 "Do not let your hearts be troubled. Trust in God; trust also in Me."

DESPAIR

2 Corinthians 4: 8 We are hard pressed on every side, but not crushed; perplexed, but not in despair; persecuted, but not abandoned; struck down but not destroyed.

PRAYER

I trust you when the storms are here
Many times You have said, "Do not fear";
You are my peace and my delight.

PRAYER SONG

I TRUST YOU LORD

You bid me trust You Lord
When the storms of life are here
When adversities prevail
I know that You are near.

You bid me trust You Lord
And to bear my cross each day
For 'tis in my perseverance
That You will show the way.

6th September 2000

I saw Jesus walking along a cliff top and could see Him clearly, but became disturbed when I saw a crown of thorns on His head. I caught up with Him and He guided me to the top of the mountain. There He told me to look down. I saw a white heat and heard screaming. Jesus said, "I died to save you, so that you may live and be taken up in glory to My Father." I fell on my knees before Jesus and wept.

Jesus said, "Rise up, do not weep child." And He was gone. I was aware of gentleness lifting my body and guiding me away from the fiery pit.

INTERPRETATION

Jesus is my salvation. He is the redemptor of my sins. He died for my sins so that if I repented and turned away from sin I would be taken up in glory and would live in eternity with Him.

KEYWORDS

Salvation, Glory, Hell

SCRIPTURES

REDEMPTION

Ephesians 1: 7 In Him we have redemption through His blood, the forgiveness of sins, in accordance with the riches of God's grace.

Colossians 1: 13-14 For He has rescued us from the dominion of darkness and brought us into the kingdom of the Son He loves, in whom we have redemption, the forgiveness of sins.

HELL
Matthew 5: 22 "But I tell you that anyone who is angry with his brother will be subject to judgement. Again, anyone who says to his brother, 'Raca' is answerable to the Sanhedrin. But anyone, who says, 'You fool!' will be in danger of the fire of hell."

PRAYER

You wore on Your head
The crown of redemption
For sinners just like me
You were nailed to a tree
I weep in repentance
And I thank You Lord
I am free.

PRAYER SONG

FIX YOUR EYES ON JESUS

    Fix your eyes on Jesus
Our Lord who wore a crown
    Fix your eyes on Jesus
He lives on hallowed ground.

    Fix your eyes on Jesus
Our Lord who was nailed to a tree
    Fix your eyes on Jesus
    And live in victory.

    Fix your eyes on Jesus
  He died to forgive our sins
    Fix your eyes on Jesus
  His Kingdom you'll enter in.

    Fix your eyes on Jesus
  Of our sins we must repent
    Fix your eyes on Jesus
  And believe that He was sent.

    Fix your eyes on Jesus
  His word can set you free
    Fix your eyes on Jesus
   And live in eternity.

29ᵗʰ October 2000

"Hello Jesus," I said.

"Hello child," Jesus replied.

We walked until we came to a river. Either side of the river were fields of green, tall trees and blue sky. Jesus remarked, "See how blue is the reflection on the river. The river is also very deep and so My love for you is deep."

We walked on and came upon a young lamb. Jesus said, "Go and look after my sheep."

Jesus motioned me to follow Him. We came upon a sunlit glade and Jesus pointed to the sun, saying, "My Father created the sun for the earth to thrive and all who dwell in it. Do you think He is not able to look after one of them?"

INTERPRETATION

This walk was truly amazing! The way that the Lord told me of His love for me taught me more about His character. Jesus wasn't content with telling me that He loved me but how DEEP His love was. I was to go out into the world and give that same love.

KEYWORDS

Water, Deep, Love, Green fields.

SCRIPTURES

WATER & GREEN FIELDS

Psalm 23: 2 He makes me lie down in green pastures, He leads me beside quiet waters.

LOVE

Ephesians 2: 4 But because of His great love for us, God, who is rich in mercy, made us alive with Christ even when we were dead in transgressions — it is by grace you have been saved.

PRAYER

Dear Jesus, thank You for telling

of Your deep love for me.

You told me this in a vision

but I am blessed to be able to read it

every day in Your word (Bible).

16 November 2000

"Hello Jesus," I said.

"Hello child," Jesus replied.

We walked along a woodland path and Jesus turned and started to climb up a very steep incline like a young gazelle. Jesus called to me, "Come child, it is not much further." I struggled, I slipped, and I fell and grazed myself — but finally made it to the top. Jesus pointed below and said, "See, all of this I have laid before you."

What I saw took my breath away. I could hardly believe that we were looking down on such a beautiful world. This must be *heaven on earth, the 'New Earth'. There was no death and no sickness. Wild animals and children were playing together. Everything was born of love.*

INTERPRETATION

The Lord showed me the glory of the 'New Earth' (Revelation Chapters 21 and 22). We would have many trials in this age but the age to come heralded a new life where there were no problems at all. For instance, no conflicts of any kind, no jealousy, no bitterness, no anger, in fact no negativity or darkness at all.

KEYWORDS

Trials, Rewards

SCRIPTURES

TRIALS
James 1: 2 Consider it pure joy my brothers, whenever you face trials of many kinds, because you know that the testing of your faith develops perseverance.

REWARD

Revelation 22: 12 "Behold I am coming soon! My reward is with Me."

A PRAYER

Dear Father, thank You for bringing me

through each trial and tribulation.

Sometimes in the suffering I often thought

that You had left me, but I am learning

that You are forever watching over me.

Thank You Lord Jesus.

22nd November 2000

We walked and came upon a wide and fast-flowing river. There were large stepping-stones that stretched across to the other side. Jesus was already making His way across. I looked down and to my amazement each stone was dry. I started to cross and quickly reached the other side.

Once on the other side I was faced with a vertical grassy bank. Jesus was standing at the top. "This is the last hurdle," He said.

INTERPRETATION

I had already made up my mind that I would cross to the other side of the river before I realised that the stones were dry. The fact that the stones were dry was another indication to me that Jesus always prepares the way if you are in His will.

KEYWORDS

Water, Faith, Preparation, Spiritual growth

SCRIPTURES

WATER
Psalm 23: 2 He makes me lie down in green pastures, He leads me beside quiet waters.

PREPARATION
Ephesians 2: 10 For we are God's workmanship, created in Christ Jesus to do good works, which God prepared in advance for us to do.

FAITH
Matthew 9: 28-31 Then He touched their eyes and said, "According to your faith will it be done to you"; and

their sight was restored. Jesus warned them sternly; "See that no one knows about this." But they went out and spread the news about Him all over the region.

SPIRITUAL GROWTH

Colossians 1: 9-12 For this reason, since the day we heard about you, we have not stopped praying for you and asking God to fill you with the knowledge of His will through all spiritual wisdom and understanding. And we pray this in order that you may live a life worthy of the Lord and may please Him in every way: bearing fruit in every good work, growing in the knowledge of God, being strengthened with all power according to His glorious might, so that you may have great endurance and patience, and joyfully giving thanks to the Father, who has qualified you to share in the inheritance of the saints in the kingdom of light.

PRAYER

FAITH

Faith I have in You Lord

In that I crave full measure

To trust You and depend

Means I will store up treasure.

PRAYER SONG

I SIT AT YOUR FEET LORD

I sit at Your feet Lord
And there lies my peace
I gaze at Your face
And behold Your grace

Chorus:
Resting in You Jesus
This is the key
Following You Lord
Helps me to see.

I read Your Word Lord
And it penetrates deep
It helps me move forward
Your commandments to keep.
Chorus

Faith I must have Lord
In Your Word and Name
To build up my life, Lord
In Jesus, the same.
Chorus.

25th November 2000

Jesus and I were in a beautiful garden. I reached out my hand to touch the roses and Jesus warned that I might prick myself. I reached out to touch some other very beautiful flowers and once again Jesus warned, "Do not touch them, they are poisonous."

Jesus' words went deep into my spirit.

INTERPRETATION

Jesus once again taught me discernment. In life one must not trust oneself to everybody. There are those who treat you well at first and you warm to them, but as time goes on you realise that their tongues are poison.

KEYWORDS

Beauty, Poison, Discernment

SCRIPTURES

BEAUTY
Proverbs 31: 30 Charm is deceptive, and beauty is fleeting; but a woman who fears the Lord is to be praised.

POISON
James 3: 8 But no man can tame the tongue. It is a restless evil, full of deadly poison.

DISCERNMENT
Proverbs 28: 11 A rich man may be wise in his own eyes, but a poor man who has discernment sees through him.

Proverbs 15: 14 The discerning heart seeks knowledge, but the mouth of a fool feeds on folly.

Proverbs 17: 24 A discerning man keeps wisdom in view, but a fool's eyes wander to the ends of the earth.

PRAYER VERSES

HOLY SPIRIT

Holy Spirit please come to me
Search me out and set me free
I give my life to You right now
This to You my heartfelt vow.

Please work in me Lord
A faithful heart
Keep me from going astray
It would be a sin to part
From Yours the loving way.

Please work in me Lord
An obedient soul
Teach me to recognise
That You're in control
Yours the loving way.

Please work in me Lord
A joyful heart
Let me step forward
With joy to impart
Yours the loving way.

12 November 2000

I walked for a short while and then sat down by the roadside. I saw Jesus coming and my heart leapt. As He approached He said, "Come child," and reached out for my hand. I felt strength and warm comfort from His fingers. We walked on a grassy bank, which led down to a sandy beach where there were many fishing boats. I looked back to enjoy the view and as I surveyed the scene my eyes caught sight of the sand where we had been walking. I noticed that there was only one set of footprints and they were mine. I mentioned *this to Jesus. He said, "I am Spirit; I only come in this form [pointing to His body] so that you can see Me."*

INTERPRETATION

I had not thought of Jesus as appearing to me in spirit form, when I had these visions, but of course it made so much sense that He did.

KEYWORD

Spirit

SCRIPTURES

THE SPIRIT
John 4: 24 God is Spirit and His worshippers must worship Him in spirit and in truth. (NIV & Str. R. Bible)

20th January 2001

"Hello Jesus," I said, "forgive me for being away so long. I am unhappy. Thank You for the prompting of Your Spirit for me to seek You out."
We walked, Jesus and I, and made our way into a forest with the tallest trees I had ever seen. There was a shaft of sunlight coming through the trees and it made a pathway. Jesus pointed to the light and said, "See the sun's light — that is the path you must follow."

KEYWORDS

Son, Light, Path

INTERPRETATION

This walk spoke realms to me. The 'sun's light' I saw as Jesus, the Son — the light of the world and the path as the Word of the Lord. I had lost my way and Jesus was gently reminding me to stay on course.

SCRIPTURES

SON
1 John 4: 9 This is how God showed His love among us: He sent His one and only Son into the world that we might live through Him.

LIGHT
Psalm 27: 1 The Lord is my light and my salvation whom shall I fear? The Lord is the stronghold of my life – of whom shall I be afraid.?
Psalm 56: 13 For You have delivered me from death and my feet from stumbling.

PATH
Psalm 119: 105 Your Word is a lamp to my feet and a light for my path.
Proverbs 15: 24 The path of life leads upwards for the wise, to keep him from going down to the grave.
Isaiah 26: 7 The path of the righteous is level, O upright One, You make the way of the righteous smooth.
Psalm 23: 3 He restores my soul, He guides me in paths of righteousness for His name's sake.
Proverbs 3: 6 In all your ways acknowledge Him and He will make your paths straight.

PRAYER SONG

LOST AND FOUND

I *like* it with You Lord
You're good for my soul
My spirit rejoices
When You're in control.

Chorus:
When I am lost Lord
Show me your cross
Give me release Lord
Show me your peace.

24th January 2001

I met with Jesus and He said, "Come, child." We walked through an apple orchard. Jesus picked an apple off a tree and showed it to me. "See, this piece of fruit is without blemish." He picked another apple off the tree and pointed to the destruction caused by worms. "Do not let anything eat into you, child," He said.

We came upon a lemon grove, and Jesus said, "Be careful — watch out for acid tongues."

I asked Jesus what I should do about a group that had been spiteful to me. Jesus replied, "Let it be child; they are full of unbelief."

INTERPRETATION

I asked the question about the group because they had been quite vitriolic in their attack on my book, *Tears Behind Closed Doors*. The book has helped thousands of people return to good health.

I had had many hostile letters in the past whilst carrying out the research for the thyroid project and I had always ignored them. Jesus' answer was the confirmation I needed that I was doing the right thing by ignoring the hostility.

KEYWORDS
Acid tongues, Unbelief

SCRIPTURES

ACID TONGUES
Psalm 39: 1 I said, I will watch my ways and keep my tongue from sin; I will put a muzzle over my mouth as long as the wicked are in my presence.

UNBELIEF
2 Corinthians 6: 14 Do not be yoked together with unbelievers. For what do righteousness and wickedness have in common?
Hebrews 3: 18-19 And to whom did God swear that they would never enter His rest if not to those who disobeyed? So we see that they were not able to enter because of their unbelief.

PRAYER

Dear Jesus, help me to share Your name
with unbelievers
And to plant the seed of hope
into their souls.
Please Holy Spirit, present to me a moment
When I can impart Your love.
Many times unbelievers cry out
For lack of love.
When they think that all is lost
Help me take them to Your precious Word.

HOPE
Isaiah 40: 31 But those who hope in the Lord will renew their strength. They will soar on wings like eagles; they will run and not grow weary, they will walk and not faint.

25th January 2001

"I love You, heavenly Father," I said. "I love you child. Come, let me show you something," Jesus replied. We walked quickly along a path and my feet barely touched the ground. Although we were on a high ledge I felt safe and happy with Jesus. We reached the top and to my distress there was a young lamb caught up in some briar. Jesus quickly freed the animal and then turned to me. He said, "Whenever you come across any of My lambs who are trapped — free them."
"Yes Lord," I answered.

INTERPRETATION

I knew that the thyroid project that I was involved in was helping people to return to good health. The medical profession rely totally on thyroid blood test results instead of taking into account signs, symptoms, patient history and carrying out a clinical appraisal. Several decades ago such thorough examination was the norm. Many people are slipping through the net and are not correctly diagnosed with a thyroid problem; instead they are pigeon-holed into another disease or condition. I have been raising awareness of this problem for eleven years now.

KEYWORDS

Trapped, Free, Help

SCRIPTURES

TRAPPED
Psalm 146: 7 He upholds the cause of the oppressed and gives food to the hungry. The Lord sets prisoners free, the Lord gives sight to the blind, lifts up those who are bowed down, the Lord loves the righteous.

MY PRAYER FOR YOU

If you shut the door

And do not share your grief with the Father

He can offer no comfort

Because you block His care

THE FATHER FEELS YOUR PAIN

He is patient and will wait for you

To open the door and welcome Him in.

24th April 2001

I came to my quiet time with Jesus in an anxious state today.

I met with Jesus. I asked Him if the second edition of my book would be published.
"Child," He replied, "you will reach the heights, but lessons have to be learned first. Go and rest in My pleasure."

KEYWORDS

Instruction, The Word

INTERPRETATION

This book is like a journey. Jesus' gentleness of spirit and His deep love for me have won my heart and I want to be in His will. Along the way, the journey offers correction, teaching, rebuking and love, most of all love. Through these walks I have seen many facets of Jesus, and Scripture backs up each walk. I want to be moulded into the person that Jesus wants me to be, and not the person I would like to be.

SCRIPTURES

INSTRUCTION

Proverbs 8: 33-36 (Wisdom's call) Listen to my instruction and be wise: do not ignore it. Blessed is the man who listens to me, watching daily at my doors, waiting at my doorway. For whoever finds me finds life and receives favour from the Lord. But whoever fails to find me harms himself; all who hate me love death.

PRAYER SONG

As I seek Your face
You show me grace
In bountiful measure
As I sit at Your feet
'Tis there that we meet
All this do I treasure.

Chorus:
Each day I give my life to You
Each day I give my life anew.

You teach me through Your Word Lord
With this I can move forward
In bountiful measure
Fresh revelations come
May Your will be done
All this do I treasure.

Chorus:
Each day I give my life to You
Each day I give my life anew.

10th May 2001

I gave to the Lord in prayer the thyroid project, counselling of thyroid sufferers, and writing. With regard to the counselling of thyroid sufferers I had burned myself out. Of course I had been working in my own strength. I needed guidance from the Lord for His will in all of this.

I met with Jesus and walked with Him until we came to a bluebell wood. Jesus said, "Sit down, child, and rest. All who come to Me heavy-laden I will give them rest."

INTERPRETATION

The Lord was once again telling me to rest in Him. It came to me that once the second edition of *Tears Behind Closed Doors* was published, then the majority of the answers to the questions posed by the sufferers were to be found in the book. Thank you Jesus.

KEYWORDS
Rest, Guidance

SCRIPTURES
REST
Psalm 91: 1
> He who dwells in the shelter of the Most High will rest in the shadow of the Almighty.

PRAYER SONG

GUIDANCE

Show me Your ways Lord
And guide me in truth.
Teach me Your paths Lord
My hope is in You.
Turn to me now Lord
With Your gracious ways
In You I trust
For the rest of my days.

19th May 2001

I met with Jesus on a hill. With a great sweep of His arms He said, "See all He has done; will He not do for you?"

KEYWORDS

Creation, Wonder

INTERPRETATION

The Lord was saying to me if I had faith He would give me my heart's desire.

It is May 2005 and I am typing up my manuscript for the publishers. As I sit here in my home — 'Swallow Lodge' — I thank the Lord. He gave me my heart's desire. I asked many years ago for a view from my home, the trees, the birds and a sunset and I have them all and more — I see the sunrise.

Back to 2001

SCRIPTURES

WONDERS

Psalm 136: 4 Give thanks to the Lord of lords! His love endures for ever. To Him who alone does great wonders. His love endures for ever.

Daniel 4: 3 How great are His signs and how mighty His wonders! His kingdom is an everlasting kingdom. And His dominion is from generation to generation. (NKJ)

PRAYER SONG

ROBIN SONG

I hear Your song of the morning Lord
Calling out to me
The distant cries of all that flies
And the robin sings for me.

O Lord I see You care
Your beauty is everywhere
From stately tree to delicate flower
And I take rest 'neath that very bower.

PRAYER

WONDERS

I marvel at all the wonders
That You alone have created
Dear Lord I stand in awe
Of Your mercy and faithfulness
And I come before Your throne of grace
With all of me and nothing less.

22nd May 2001

Jesus and I walked over the hills, which were covered in tall grasses, together with bright blue and yellow flowers. It was a magnificent sight! I felt the pleasure of Jesus and His warmth on a gentle summer breeze. I asked for guidance for the day. Jesus said, "Be not hurried, hasten not; go and enjoy."

INTERPRETATION

When we hurry too much and are busy, busy, we miss so much in life because we fill it with unrealistic goals and targets that are sometimes impossible to reach. Some of the goals are set for us and some we set for ourselves. Realistic goals that challenge us are good, but unrealistic goals cause unwanted stress.

KEYWORDS

Time to enjoy

SCRIPTURES

TIME

Ecclesiastes 5: 18-20 Here is what I have seen: it is good and fitting for one to eat and drink and to enjoy the good of all his labour in which he toils under the sun all the days of his life which God gives him; for it is his heritage. (NKJ)

PRAYER

O Lord I pray that I will take time to enjoy

Your creation,

And to enjoy the fruits of my labour.

I will take time just to be

And rest awhile when my body tells me so.

7th July 2001

I walked until I saw Jesus. He pointed to the trees and the water and said, "See, child, how the sunlight dances through the trees and look as the sun rests on the water, see how she brings forth jewels as she dances her delight."

INTERPRETATION

Jesus gives joy to my heart. Jesus is joy. He is the giver of all good things. He gave His life for me! Jesus humbled himself for me. He came from a place of exaltation to a place of lowliness. How can I doubt Him? He gave His life so that I may have life in abundance and that it may be filled with joy, His joy.

KEYWORDS
Give, Joy

SCRIPTURES

GIVE

Psalm 37: 4 Delight yourself also in the Lord, and He will give you the desires of your heart.
John 10: 11 I am the good shepherd. The good shepherd gives his life for the sheep. (NKJ)

JOY

Jeremiah 15: 16 Your words were found, and I ate them, and Your word was to me the joy and rejoicing of my heart. (NKJ)
John 15: 11 These things I have spoken to you, that My joy may remain in you, and that your joy may be full. (NKJ)
Psalm 16: 11 You will show me the path of life; in Your presence is fullness of joy. At Your right hand are pleasures forevermore. (NKJ)

PRAYER SONG

JOY

Joy has filled my heart

Which is sent from heaven above

Never more to part

From Jesus whom I love.

Jesus is my anchor

Always there for me

By seeking Him every day

Then will I see.

22nd August 2001

Jesus was looking down at me but I could not see His face. He was all light. I had walked a long way to search for Him and now I was faced with a small hill to climb before I could reach Him. The walk ended abruptly.

INTERPRETATION

Were the obstacles of my own making? Was there anything blocking the way to the Lord? Why couldn't I reach Him? One thing I knew for sure — the Lord was always there for me and He hadn't deserted me. I had seen Him in all His glory in the vision and He was letting me know that He would always be there. Thank You Jesus.

KEYWORDS

Searching, Obstacles, Light

SCRIPTURES

SEARCHING

1 Corinthians 2: 10 But God has revealed it to us by His Spirit. The Spirit searches all things, even the deep things of God.

LIGHT

Matthew 5: 14 You are the light of the world. A city that is set on a hill cannot be hidden.

PRAYER

There's pain in my life, but You're guiding me through
O Jesus my Saviour I'm lost without You
You're always there, there at my side
O Father God 'tis with You I'll abide.

A feeling, a knowing and Your guiding light
Brings to my mind just how awesome Your might
Jesus to me You are the giver of life
And always You're there, my Helper through strife.

8th November 2001

I walked through a wood and saw Jesus resting by a tree.
It was autumn and the sun shone on the brightly coloured leaves. "Come walk with me child," said Jesus. We walked a little way, and then Jesus stopped and sat down on a log. He motioned to me to sit with Him and pointed to the brightly coloured leaves, saying, "Life is colourful." He then moved the leaves, which showed up the dark earth beneath and said, "Sometimes there are dark times in life, but you will come through these times and then all will be colourful again."

INTERPRETATION

At this particular time in my life I had been humiliated and Jesus was saying to me: It will pass, and you will overcome all that has happened to you and all that will happen to you in the future. And I believe this to be so. Jesus' Word is light and life to me.

KEYWORDS

Overcome, Light, Dark

SCRIPTURES

OVERCOME

John 16: 33 "These things I have spoken to you, that in Me you may have peace. In the world you will have tribulation, but be of good cheer, I have overcome the world." (ST. R. B.)
Revelation 2: 11 "He who has an ear, let him hear what the Spirit says to the churches. He who overcomes shall not be hurt by the second death." (NKJ)
Revelation 21: 7 "He who overcomes shall inherit all things, and I will be His God and he shall be My son." (NKJ)

DARK

2 Samuel 22: 29 For You are my lamp O Lord; the Lord shall enlighten my darkness. (NKJ)

LIGHT

Psalm 27: 1 The Lord is my light and my salvation; whom shall I fear? The Lord is the strength of my life; of whom shall I be afraid? (NKJ)

Psalm 118: 27 God is the Lord and He has given us light. (NKJ)

Isaiah 2: 5 O house of Jacob, come let us walk in the light of the Lord. (NKJ)

Revelation 21: 23 The city had no need of the sun or of the moon to shine in it, for the glory of God illuminated it. The Lamb is its light. (NKJ)

PRAYER SONG

In the light of my Lord
My salvation has come
With the double-edged sword
Jesus, my Saviour, has won.

Chorus:
Jesus Lord of my heart
My life I give to Thee
Never more to part
Because I want to be free.

His light is shining bright
His glory all around
Jesus shows His might
If in Him we abound.

Chorus:
Jesus Lord of my heart
My life I give to Thee
Never more to part
Because I want to be free.

13th December 2001

I started my music, turned down the volume; and called to Jesus.

JESUS

JESUS

Would He be there? Yes, there He was, but there was a raging river between us, with Jesus on the far bank.

Jesus beckoned. I looked to the right and the left and noticed a bridge on the left. I also noticed a log stretching right across the river. I looked at Jesus. He beckoned me again. I knew instinctively that He wanted me to walk out in faith across the water. I did this, and

when I reached the other side Jesus said, "You have taken a step in faith." Then He was gone.

KEYWORD

Faith

INTERPRETATION

While out to lunch with a friend I was convicted by the Holy Spirit. There was an issue, in our marriage, between my husband and me, and the Holy Spirit was urging me to make the first move. I was to ask my husband to forgive me for not forgiving him. I did ask my husband's forgiveness although it was not easy. Of course there was an easier option open to me; I could have done nothing and saved myself the humiliation, but that would not have helped my marriage! I knew that Jesus was asking me to die to self.

SCRIPTURES

FAITH

Hebrews 11: 1 Now faith is being sure of what we hope for and certain of what we do not see.

Hebrews 11: 3 By faith we understand that the universe was formed at God's command, so that what is seen is not made out of what is visible.

Mark 11: 22-24 So Jesus answered and said to them, "Have faith in God, for assuredly, I say to you, whoever says to this mountain, 'Be removed and cast into the sea,' and does not doubt in his heart, but believes that those things he says will be done, he will have whatever he says. Therefore I say to you, whatever things you ask when you pray, believe that you receive them, and you will have them." (NKJ)

A PRAYER OF FAITH

In my prayers, I ask You Lord
Please, to give me more faith
Faith to be bold, faith to go forward
Faith in the Spirit I do not see
Faith in full measure
That will bring me such treasure
And then will I know I am free.

3rd August 2002

JESUS

JESUS

It was some time before Jesus came. I ran to Him; He enfolded me in His arms and said, "Come." I followed Him. We walked for some time and then Jesus sat on a rock.
"Come and sit with Me," He said. We surveyed the scene together. It was so beautiful. Jesus turned and said, "I have given you many gifts. Go and use them."

INTERPRETATION

My understanding of the gifts was both spiritual and temporal.

KEYWORDS

Temporal gifts, Spiritual gifts, Holy Spirit, Baptism in the Spirit, Gift of tongues.

SPIRITUAL

I have the gift of faith, and discerning the spirits. I also have the gift of wisdom to a lesser degree although I have asked the Father for more of this gift. I have the gift of encouragement, which I know builds people up. We all need encouragement. I also have the gift of other tongues.

There are those who believe that to be 'born again' you must be able to speak in tongues. I do not believe this to be scriptural.

For years I was made to believe that I was a second-class Christian because I couldn't speak in a different tongue. I was made to feel inferior and Leaders and Pastors from different churches tried to force me to speak in tongues. I read and re-read Paul's words in Corinthians and nowhere does he state that you must be able to speak in a different tongue to become 'born again'. The scriptures relate the truth.

TEMPORAL

My temporal gifts are: singing, painting and writing. I am truly blessed!

SCRIPTURES

1 CORINTHIANS 12: 4-10 THE NINE GIFTS OF THE SPIRIT ARE:
The word of wisdom
The word of knowledge
Faith
Gifts of healing
The working of miracles
Prophecy
Discerning of spirits
Different kinds of tongues
The interpretation of tongues

GIFTS OF THE SPIRIT

Romans 12: 3-8 By the grace given me I say to every one of you: do not think of yourself more highly than you ought, but rather think of yourself with sober judgement, in accordance with the measure of faith God has given you. Just as each one of us has one body with many members; these members _do not all have the same function_, so in Christ we who are many form one body, and each member belongs to all the others. We have _different gifts, according to the grace given us._ If a man's gift is prophesying, let him use it in proportion to his faith. If it is serving, let him serve; if it is teaching, let him teach; if it is encouraging, let him encourage; if it is contributing to the needs of others, let him give generously; if it is leadership, let him govern diligently; if it is showing mercy, let him do it cheerfully.

GIFT OF TONGUES

1 Corinthians 12: 4-31 There are different kinds of gifts, but the same Spirit. There are different kinds of service, but the same Lord. There are different kinds of working, but the same God works all of them in all men. Now to each one the manifestation of the Spirit is given for the common good. **To one** there is given through the Spirit the message of wisdom, **to another** the message of knowledge by means of the same Spirit, **to another** faith by the same Spirit, **to another** gifts of healing by that one Spirit, **to another** miraculous powers, **to another** prophecy, **to another** distinguishing between spirits, **to another** speaking in different kinds of tongues, and to still **another** the interpretation of tongues. All these are the work of one and the same Spirit, and He gives them to each one, just **as He determines.**

1 Corinthians chapter 14.

I urge you to read this chapter over and over to capture the reality of Paul's words.

PRAYER

I pray Lord, for those who do not speak in another tongue. I pray that no one tries to force what can only be a gift from You. Let no one ridicule them. I know the pain and the hurt that this entails. I pray for understanding for all.

PRAYER

Thank You for these gifts Lord
For I know that they come from You.
It is written in Your Word
that we accept them too.

PRAYER SONG

Jesus Lord; light of my life
Clothe me in grace
And show Your face
To those who do not see.

Jesus Lord; let Your love reign
And fill me to overflowing
Let all people see that they want to be
Like You just from the knowing.

16th August 2002

Jesus was standing on a stony pathway. Suddenly the wind blew and His robes lifted and His hair blew freely in the wind.

Jesus said, "The wind blows and no one knows whence it comes. And so it is with the Holy Spirit."

HOLY SPIRIT OF JESUS CHRIST MY FATHER – THREE IN ONE

INTERPRETATION

The Spirit of God moves without and within us and we do not know when His stirring will come upon us. The Spirit of the Lord inspires us to move when the time is right. It is our responsibility to be ready for that time.

The Word of the Lord is our template

KEYWORDS

Holy Spirit, the Word

HOLY SPIRIT

John 6: 63 "The Spirit gives life; the flesh counts for nothing. The words I have spoken to you are spirit and they are life."

THE WORD

John 1: 1 & 14 In the beginning was the Word, and the Word was with God, and the Word was God. **Verse 14:** And the Word became flesh and dwelt among us, and we beheld His glory, the glory as of the only begotten of the Father, full of grace and truth. (NKJ)

Hebrews 4: 12 For the Word of God is living and powerful, and sharper than any two-edged sword, piercing even to the division of soul and spirit, and of joints and marrow, and is a discerner of the thoughts and intents of the heart. (NKJ)

2 Samuel 22: 31 As for God, His way is perfect. The Word of the Lord is proven; He is a shield to all who trust in Him. (NKJ)

Psalm 119: 11 Your Word I have hidden in my heart, that I might not sin against You. (NKJ)

Psalm: 119: 105 Your Word is a lamp to my feet and a light to my path. (NKJ)

PRAYER SONG

I lift my eyes to You Lord
To You upon the throne
All majesty personified
You are God alone.

I lift my eyes to You Lord
In reverence and in love
Your Word and name I worship
O God in heaven above.

23rd August 2002

Suddenly light shone and there was Jesus. The birds were singing, water was flowing and harps were being played.
Jesus walked on a higher path, and no matter how hard I tried I couldn't reach Him. I stopped being in earnest about it and walked on the lower path, and amazingly very soon we were together. In front of us was a door, very overgrown with weeds. Jesus opened the door and led me into a garden that was choked of life because of so many weeds. Jesus said, "There is one close to

you who is choked with weeds of the past; but I am the Master gardener."

KEYWORDS

The past

INTERPRETATION

I knew who the Lord was talking about and I prayed that that person would be healed.

SCRIPTURE

Isaiah 43: 18 Forget the former things; do not dwell on the past.

PRAYER SONG

Show me Your ways Lord
And guide me in truth
Teach me Your paths Lord
My hope is in You.

Take care of me Lord
With Your gracious ways
In You I trust
For the rest of my days.

12th October 2002

I prayed to the Lord for more love, patience, tolerance and forgiveness. I closed my eyes and called to Jesus.

Jesus came into my vision. He was standing next to a waterfall and pointing to it. I was there for some time watching Him and then it suddenly dawned on me: Jesus was reminding me of the 'rivers of living water'.

INTERPRETATION
The Lord's Word is the very sustenance that my soul needs. If I am bathed in this more and more, the rivers of living water will pour out of me in the form of love, patience, tolerance, and forgiveness. I know now that the more one reads the Word the more the mind-set changes, and if I really want to be Christ-like this is something that I must do.

KEYWORD

Water

SCRIPTURES

John 7: 38 "He who believes in Me, as the Scripture has said, out of his heart will flow rivers of living water." (NKJ)

John 4: 14 "But whoever drinks of the water that I shall give him will never thirst. But the water that I shall give him will become in him a fountain of water springing up into everlasting life." (NKJ)

PRAYER SONG

O dearest Lord You give to me
Rivers of living water
Cleansing sin so thoroughly
You are the very life to me.

CHORUS
Rivers of water living in me
Rivers of water setting me free
Rivers of water I want to be
Bathed in Christ Jesus and live eternally.

22nd October 2002

Prayer to Jesus

Dear Jesus, today I met with Your Word,

which related to me

that if I neglect your Word I neglect You

and if I neglect You I neglect myself

and therefore cannot be built up in You

and grow in Your likeness.

KEYWORD

The Word

SCRIPTURES

Hebrews 2: 1-3 Therefore we must give more earnest heed to the things we have heard, lest we drift away. For if the Word spoken through angels proved steadfast, and every transgression and disobedience received a just reward, how shall we escape if we neglect so great a salvation, which at the first began to be spoken by the Lord, and was confirmed to us by those who heard Him. (NKJ)

Psalm 119: 16 I will delight myself in Your statutes; I will not forget Your Word. (NKJ)

PRAYER SONG

Holy Spirit take me to a place
Where I can be refreshed
Take me to a place where
I can rise above each test.

Guide me through the hurt
Of the happenings of the day
And fill me full of love
And be with me when I pray.

Do not let me drift away
Bring me help on angels' wings
That will give to me new heart
Then I will truly sing.

18th November 2002

This particular morning I was very anxious. My marriage was still in trouble and I had taken out a loan for the second edition of my book *Tears Behind Closed Doors* so that I could publish it myself. I did not like owing money even though my motive was good; I was still concerned about it. The first edition sold out and I know that the majority of those people were helped in one way or another.

I went into prayer

I called to Jesus.

JESUS

JESUS

JESUS

Jesus appeared.
"Why are you troubled?" He said.
"My marriage is failing, and I owe money so that I can publish the book," I replied.
"Where is your faith?" said Jesus.

INTERPRETATION

Where indeed was my faith? When I am anxious or disturbed the first thing I should do is to go to the Word of God. It is there that I will find the answers and the comfort.

KEYWORDS

Faith, Troubled, Worry

SCRIPTURES

FAITH

Matthew 9: 28-29 And when He had come into the house, the blind men came to Him. And Jesus said to them, "Do you believe that I am able to do this?" They said to Him, "Yes Lord." Then He touched their eyes, saying, "According to your faith let it be to you." (NKJ)

Mark 11: 22 So Jesus answered and said to them, "Have faith in God." (NKJ)

Romans 1: 17 For in it the righteousness of God is revealed from faith to faith; as it is written, "The just shall live by faith." (NKJ)

TROUBLED

John 14: 27 "Peace I leave with you, My peace I give to you; not as the world gives do I give to you. Let not your heart be troubled, neither let it be afraid." (NKJ)

Matthew 6: 25 "Therefore I tell you, do not worry about your life, what you will eat or drink; or about your body, what you will wear. Is not life more important than food and the body more important than clothes?"

PRAYER SONG

Faith I need to see me through
Each trial and tribulation
Faith will bring me straight to You
Without the condemnation.

A tiny seed is all I need
By faith it will mature
And with Your Word, Lord, I shall feed
And will no longer be poor.

29ᵀᴴ NOVEMBER 2002

I sat down to pray.

JESUS

JESUS

JESUS

He appeared. There was a fierce wind pulling at His robes. "Child, stand firm, the winds of change are coming." I wept.

INTERPRETATION

What did this mean? At the time I did not know. A few weeks later I found out. I had been struggling with the church that I had been attending for some time. There seemed to be no interest in those who were suffering and everyone appeared to have their own agenda. I had attended this particular church for eight years but felt that the Lord wanted me to move on. My season at that church had come to an end. The Lord decides the seasons for us.

KEYWORDS

Stand firm, Changes, Seasons

SCRIPTURES

CHANGES, SEASONS
Daniel 2: 21 And He changes the times and the seasons. He removes kings and raises up kings; He gives wisdom to the wise and knowledge to those who have understanding. (NKJ)

STAND FIRM
Ephesians 6: 14 Stand therefore, having girded your waist with truth, having put on the breastplate of righteousness. (NKJ)

PRAYER SONG

Beware the winds of change, child,
Lest they take you unaware
Do not rest in comfort zone
For 'tis then you have left My care.

Be bold and ready with My Word
And the confidence you gain
Will be My reward.

22nd December 2002

I was in that secret place again.

JESUS

JESUS

JESUS

There He was. I hurried to Him and then walked by His side. "Come with Me, child, to new pastures," said Jesus.

KEYWORDS

New pastures, Truth

INTERPRETATION

This was so relevant to me as I had just left the church I had attended for eight years. Where was the Lord going to take me?

SCRIPTURES

PSALM 23

> The Lord is my shepherd
> I shall not want
> He makes me lie down in green pastures,
> He leads me beside still waters
> He restores my soul
> He leads me in the paths of righteousness

For His name's sake
Yea, though I walk through the valley
Of the shadow of death, I will fear no evil
For You are with me
Your rod and Your staff they comfort me.
You prepare a table before me in the presence of my enemies;
You anoint my head with oil
My cup runs over.
Surely goodness and mercy will follow me
All the days of my life
And I will dwell in the house of the Lord forever.

(NKJ)

PRAYER SONG

I come to You in the secret place
I come to You to seek Your face
I come to You to learn Your ways
And I come to You to give You praise.

I come to You in simple faith
I come to You and You show me grace
I come to You on bended knee
I come to You that I might see.

8th February 2003

Someone had said some very cruel words to me and as I went before Jesus I wept.

Jesus did not appear to me today but I was before Him in silence and He impressed on me the scripture set out below:

John 15: 10-11 "If you obey My commands, you will remain in My love, just as I have obeyed My Father's commands and remain in His love. I have told you this so that My joy may be in you and that your joy may be complete. My command is this: Love each other as I have loved you."

PRAYER SONG

In that secret place
I am in Your grace
Your beauty shines so bright
You are my guiding light.

Chorus:
Dear Jesus take me into You
And let my whole life be renewed.

In that secret place
Your mercy everywhere
You clothe me with a heart that sings
And lift me up on eagles' wings.

19th June 2003

Jesus appeared and said, "Come child."

"Where to, Jesus?" I replied.

"You will see," He said.

I found myself in a very smelly passageway. Jesus was walking on ahead. I could not make out the walls or the ground beneath my feet. The stench was awful! After quite some time the passageway opened out on to a woodland pathway. The dreadful smell had disappeared and in its place was a fresh clean perfume as it is after the rain.

We continued along this path and then suddenly it opened out onto a glorious wild meadow with all kinds of beautiful wild flowers of many colours. Blues, reds, yellows, pinks, mauves, and purple, in fact every colour I could ever imagine. The sun was shining and there was a light summer breeze. There was so much light but it didn't hurt my eyes.

Jesus turned and said, "There will be heaven on earth; stay with Me child."

KEYWORDS

Dark, clean, brightness, light, joy, 'new heaven on earth'

INTERPRETATION

I believed this walk to be a warning to me of an unpleasant time to come. I did not know what form this would take or how long it would last. After the unpleasant time there would be a time of cleansing and renewing and then would come the joy.

I was to find out about the unpleasant time in December 2003 and January 2004. My husband and I had joined a church in February 2003, which we attended for 10 months. We did learn a lot at that church but some of the doctrines were strange.
    A Pastor told me that God wanted to kill me. I said, "No, that is not correct; God wants me to 'die to self', which is totally different. If God wanted to kill me then He would be taking the initiative and I would have no choice. God gave us choice! I have the choice of whether I 'die to self' or not." The Pastor insisted he was right and he said we would have to agree to differ. I was unhappy with many more issues and therefore decided to leave the church. I felt that God's truth was not in that church.

SCRIPTURES

DARK
John 3: 19 "And this is the condemnation, that the light has come into the world, and men loved darkness rather than light, because their deeds were evil." (NKJ)

CLEAN

John 15: 3 "You are already clean because of the word which I have spoken to you." (NKJ)

BRIGHTNESS

Hebrews 1: 1-3 God, who at various times and in various ways spoke in time past to the fathers by the prophets, has in these last days spoken to us by His Son, whom He has appointed heir of all things, through whom also He made the worlds; who being the brightness of His glory and the express image of His person, and upholding all things by the word of His power, when He had by Himself purged our sins, sat down at the right hand of the Majesty on high. (NKJ)

A NEW HEAVEN AND A NEW EARTH

Revelation 21: 4-5 "And God will wipe away every tear from their eyes; there shall be no more death, nor sorrow, nor crying. There shall be no more pain, for the former things have passed away." Then He who sat on the throne said, "Behold, I make all things new." And He said to me, "Write, for these words are true and faithful." (NKJ)

PRAYER

O Father, where there is darkness

Let there be light.

1st September 2003

I was in the secret place and felt the presence of Jesus. His voice came through loud and strong. "Child, do not be afraid to get your feet wet. Go forward in faith and My plan for you will be revealed."

INTERPRETATION

The Lord was encouraging me to step out in faith and He would reveal His plan. I was mystified and did not know in which area I was to step out in faith.

KEYWORDS

Faith, Courage, Fear

FEAR

2 Timothy 1: 7 For God has not given us a spirit of fear, but of power and of love and of a sound mind.

FAITH

Ephesians 6: 16 Above all, taking the shield of faith with which you will be able to quench all the fiery darts of the wicked one. (NKJ)

PRAYER SONG

In that secret place with You

My heart and mind are still

I am hushed into a lull

'Tis there I find Your will.

In that secret place with You

My cup of joy runs over

You bid me to go out in faith

And Your wings will be my cover.

20th October 2003

I bowed my head and called to Jesus.

JESUS

JESUS

JESUS

Jesus replied, "Come follow Me."
I was looking out from a darkened place onto a beautiful scene. There was light and colour with Jesus at the centre a radiant light. Jesus said, "Come into My

world — heaven, here on earth;
just follow Me."

I stepped out of the darkness into the light and the Lord said to me, "Child, you have grown."

INTERPRETATION

I took Jesus' statement to mean that I had grown spiritually. I really felt that I **had** grown. I remember the painful experiences, but now I have the key to overcome any hurt, or evil that the future holds.

KEYWORDS

Follow, Growth

SCRIPTURE

John 12: 26 "If anyone serves Me let him follow Me; and where I am, there My servant will be also. If anyone serves Me, him My Father will honour." (NKJ)

PRAYER

O Keeper of my spirit

You who teach me well

With passing time I have grown

But there is more for You to tell.

10th January 2004

I knew Jesus was waiting for me. I called out:

JESUS

JESUS

Jesus spoke, "Patience child, the time is coming soon when I will reveal My will to you."

Instantly a verse of scripture came into my mind.

Matthew 5: 16 "Let your light so shine before men that they may see your good works and glorify your Father in heaven." (NKJ)

KEYWORDS

Patience, Will

SCRIPTURES

PATIENCE
Colossians 1: 10-11 And we pray this in order that you may live a life worthy of the Lord and may please Him in every way: bearing fruit in every good work, growing in the knowledge of God, being strengthened with all power according to His glorious might, so that you may have great endurance and patience, and joyfully giving thanks to the Father, who has qualified you to share in the inheritance of the saints in the kingdom of light.

WILL
Psalm 40: 8 "I desire to do Your will, O my God; Your law is within my heart."

John 7: 17 "If anyone chooses to do God's will, he will find out whether My teaching comes from God or whether I speak on My own."

* * * * *

In January 2004 I felt the Lord urging me to leave the church I was attending. The doctrines were not the Lord's truth. Many people left at the same time. Above all else I was to seek the truth.

January 11th 2004

JESUS

JESUS

Jesus' words came through to me,
" I love you child; stay close to Me.
Break up the rubble in your life!
All will become clear. Do not fret,
child, My eye is on you."

KEYWORDS

Love, Worry, Caring

INTERPRETATION

I knew then that I was to leave the church without delay. The rubble in my life was the destruction of the Lord's truth and I had to clear out any debris that was not of the Lord. When I left the church there was a sense of relief, and a sense of loss. Relief because I was away from the lies, and loss, not from the church I had just left, but because I was without a church family. Strangely I had no sense of urgency to find another church at that time.

Although I had attended the church for just ten months I had had some good teaching and had learnt discernment to a greater degree than before. I believe that with every experience, good or bad, we can learn.

SCRIPTURES

John 14:12 "Most assuredly I say to you, he who believes in Me, the works that I do he will do also; and greater works than these will he do, because I go to My Father." (NKJ)

May 29th 2004

Although I talked with Jesus each day and I knew He was close, I had not studied His Word for weeks. I felt an urging to read more of His Word. I asked His forgiveness, closed my eyes and called to Him.

JESUS

JESUS

Jesus' voice gently pervaded my space and He said, "Come child, follow Me." We were by the water's edge. Jesus said, "The tide ebbs and flows, as in relationships. There is a drawing close and a moving away and so it goes on. There is no condemnation child. Guilt can play no part in a relationship with Me. By seeking Me you will be fulfilled."

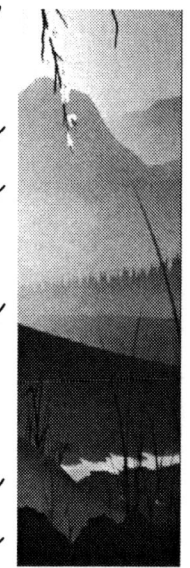

KEYWORDS

Relationships, Condemnation, Seeking, Fulfilled

INTERPRETATION

I knew that this walk was referring to my marriage.

SCRIPTURES

SEEK
Amos 5: 4 For thus says the Lord to the house of Israel: "Seek Me and live." (NKJ)

Matthew 6: 33 "But seek first the kingdom of God and His righteousness; and all these things shall be added to you." (NKJ)

PRAYER

I seek Your friendship O dear Father

Your righteousness I behold

I know that when I read Your Word

'Tis with truth I can become bold.

3rd August 2004

I was there in that secret place and Jesus said, "Come walk with Me."

We walked until we came to a very large rock. Jesus motioned me to sit beside Him.

"What is Your will for me?" I asked Jesus.

He got up and said, "Come." We came upon a young tree. It was a strange tree. One side was lifeless and the other side was healthy, vibrant and the fruit hung in masses from the branches. Jesus said, "Follow Me and your life will be fruitful."

KEYWORDS

Death, Life

INTERPRETATION

Some people will live death instead of life because they are not true believers of Jesus Christ. Others live life to the full because they live by His Word.

SCRIPTURE

DEATH & LIFE

Romans 6: 23 For the wages of sin is death; but the gift of God is eternal life in Christ Jesus our Lord. (NKJ)

PRAYER SONG

You came into my life Lord

And brought me up from death

You showed to me Your Word, Lord

Which gave to me new breath.

You taught me how to live my life

With truth set as the goal

You wash me with Your Holy Spirit

This sanctifies my soul.

The final walk for this book:

AUGUST 2004

JESUS

JESUS

JESUS

Jesus spoke: "Precious child, you are Mine."

With this particular walk no interpretation is needed. I know I belong to the Father and He is with me daily as we walk through life together. I feel His presence watching, guiding, warning, teaching and loving me through all things of life. Whether it is trials and tribulations, joy or peace in fact the Lord God is with me in every area of my life. What comfort in the knowledge that He is always there. I am never alone. For He is in me and I am in Him.

In the words of Oswald Chambers I must:

-

"Let the past rest, but let it rest in the sweet embrace of Christ. And leave the broken, irreversible past in His hands, and step out into the invincible future with Him."

The last word must rest with Jesus:

John 14: 20 *"On that day you will realise that I am in My Father, and you are in Me, and I am in you."*

SCRIPTURE REFERENCES

References are taken from the New International Version of the Bible unless indicated as follows:

New Strong's Reference Bible (ST. R. B.)
The New King James version (NKJ)

ACID TONGUES
Psalm 39: 1

BEAUTY
Proverbs 31: 30

BORN AGAIN
John 3: 7
1 Peter 1: 23

BRIGHTNESS
Hebrews 1: 1-3 (ST. R. B.)

CARRY
Exodus 19: 4

CHANGES
Daniel 2: 21 (ST.R.B.)

CLEAN
John 15: 3 (ST.R.B.)

COURAGE
Deuteronomy 31: 6

DARK/DARKNESS
2 Samuel 22: 29 (ST.R.B.)
Job 34: 22
2. Peter 1:19 (ST.R.B.)
John 3: 19

DESPAIR
2 Corinthians 4: 8

DISCIPLINE
Proverbs 3: 11; 10: 17; 12: 1; 15: 32

EMPTY
Isaiah 29: 8 (ST.R.B.)
Peter 1: 18

EVIL
Proverbs 10: 23; 11: 27; 24: 20

FAITH
Mark 11: 22
Ephesians 6: 16
2 Corinthians 5: 7
Hebrews 11: 1; 11: 3
Matthew 9: 28-31
Romans 1: 17 (NKJ)

FEAR
1. John 4: 18
Isaiah 41: 10
2 Timothy 1: 7

FELLOWSHIP
Colossians 3: 15
2 Corinthians 13: 14

GIFT OF TONGUES
1 Corinthians 12: 4-31
1 Corinthians 14 (The whole chapter)
Romans 12: 3-8

GIFTS OF THE SPIRIT
1 Corinthians 12: 4-10

GIVE
Psalm 37: 4
Matthew 6: 11 (ST.R.B.)
John 6: 27 (ST.R.B.)
John 10: 11

GLORY
Mark 8: 38

GOOD
Psalm 86: 5; 119: 68; 34: 8

GOSSIP
Proverbs 16: 28

GRACE
2 Peter 3: 18
John 1: 17
Hebrews 4: 16

HELL
Matthew 5: 22

HOLY SPIRIT
John 16: 13 (ST.R.B.)

HOPE
Proverbs 10: 28 (ST.R.B.)
Isaiah 40: 31
Romans 15: 13

HYPOCRISY
Matthew 23: 28
Psalm 26: 4

INSTRUCTION
Proverbs 8: 33-36; 16: 20; 23: 12

JOY
Jeremiah 15: 16
Psalm 16: 11; 4: 7
John 15: 11
Nehemiah 8: 10

LIGHT
Psalm 27: 1; 56: 13; 118: 27; 119: 105
Matthew 5: 14
2 Samuel 22: 29
Revelation 21: 23
Isaiah 2: 5

LOST
Luke 15: 24 (ST.R.B.)
Luke 15: 6-7

LOVE
Galatians 5: 22
2 Chronicles 5: 13
Psalm 57: 9-10
1 Corinthians 13: 4
1 John 4: 16
1 John 3: 1
Ephesians 2: 4

NEW HEAVEN ON EARTH
Revelation 21: 4-5 (ST.R.B.)

OBEY
Deuteronomy 13: 4
Acts 5: 27-29 (ST.R.B.)
Romans 2: 8 (ST.R.B. & NIV)

OVERCOME
John 16: 33 (ST.R.B.)
Revelation 2: 11; 21: 7

PAST
Isaiah 43: 18-19 (NKJ)

PATH/PATHWAYS
Psalm 23: 3; 25: 4; 27: 11; 119: 105
Proverbs 15: 24; 3: 6
Isaiah 26:7

PATIENCE
Colossians 1: 10-11 (ST.R.B.)

PEACE
Colossians 3: 15 (ST.R.B.)

PERSEVERANCE
Hebrews 12: 1
James 1: 4
Romans 5: 3-5

POISON
James 3: 8
Proverbs 15: 14; 17: 24; 28: 11

POWER
Acts 1: 8
Luke 4: 32 (ST.R.B.)

PREPARATION
Ephesians 2: 10

PROTECTION
John 17: 11
Psalm 32: 7
Psalm 91

REDEMPTION
Ephesians 1: 7
Colossians 1: 13-14

REST
Psalm 37: 7 (ST.R.B.)
Matthew 11: 29
Jeremiah 6: 16
Matthew 11: 28-29

REWARDS
Revelation 22: 12

ROOTED
Colossians 2: 7 (NKJ)
Ephesians 3: 16 (NKJ)

SEARCHING
1 Corinthians 2: 10

SON
1 John 4: 9

SPIRIT
Job 33: 4 (NKJ)
John 16: 13

STAND FIRM
Ephesians 6: 14
Job 11: 13-19

STRENGTH
Exodus 15: 2
Philippians 4: 13

TEARS
Revelation 7: 17
Psalm 126: 5

TEMPTATION
Matthew 6: 13 (NKJ)
Matthew 26: 41 (NKJ)

TESTING THE SPIRITS
1 John 4: 1

THE WAY, THE TRUTH AND THE LIFE
John 14: 6

TIME TO ENJOY
Ecclesiastes 5: 18-20 (NKJ)

TRAPPED
Psalm 146: 7

TRIALS AND TRIBULATIONS
Romans 5: 3; 12: 12 (ST.R.B.)
James 1: 2
Mark 8: 38

TROUBLED
John 14: 27
2 Corinthians 4: 8 (ST.R.B.)

TRUST
Proverbs 3: 5-6 (ST.R.B.)

Psalm 32: 10; 56: 4
Psalm 7: 10 (ST.R.B.)
John 14: 1

TRUTH
John 16: 13 (NKJ)

UNBELIEF
Hebrews 3: 18-19
Romans 3: 3

WATER
 John 4: 14
John 7: 38
Revelation 21: 6

WATER & GREEN FIELDS
Psalm 23: 2

WILL
Psalm 40: 8
John 7: 17

WONDERS
Psalm 136
Daniel 4: 3 (ST.R.B.)

WORD OF GOD
2 Samuel 22: 31
Psalm 119: 11,16,105; 130: 5 (ST.R.B.)
John 1: verses 1 & 14 (ST.R.B.)

Hebrews 2: 1-3; 4: 12 (ST.R.B.)
James 1: 25 (ST.R.B.)

WORLD
John 15: 19

WORRY
Matthew 6: 25